CELTIC TREE RITUALS

© Giacomo Tosti

About the Author

Sharlyn Hidalgo has an MA in psychology, and although she is now in semiretirement, she is a practicing astrologer, tarot reader, teacher, healer, artist, and author. She has worked as a counselor for an agency and in private practice.

Because of her Celtic roots and her love for trees, she is enamored with the ancient spiritual practices of the British Isles. She is author of *The Healing Power of Trees: Spiritual Journeys through the Celtic Tree Calendar*, through Llewellyn Publications, and tree cards entitled *Celtic Tree Oracle*, through Blue Angel publications (illustrated by Jimmy Manton).

Sharlyn teaches classes on the Celtic trees, runs a yearly Druid apprenticeship, and holds ceremonies that celebrate the turning of the wheel in the Celtic native European tradition.

She also teaches classes on tarot and astrology, mandalas and creativity, dreamwork, and mind treatments via Science of Mind and Ernest Holmes. She is dedicated to protecting nature and promoting peace and healing on our planet.

She is certified, through Nicki Scully, as a practitioner and teacher of Alchemical Healing, an energetic healing form sourced in Egypt. Sharlyn has been to Egypt eight times and led three successful tours to Egypt. She has written a book about her experiences there, entitled *Nazmy: Love Is My Religion: Egypt, Travel, and a Quest for Peace* with a foreword by Jean Houston, and teaches classes on the Egyptian Mysteries. She is currently completing her novel (magical realism): *The Daughter of Unas, A Spiritual Sojourn: The Healing Power of Past Lives in Egypt*.

She can be found online at alchemicalhealingarts.com and her blog alchemicalhealingarts.blogspot.com.

CEREMONIES
FOR THE THIRTEEN
MOON MONTHS
AND A DAY

CELTIC TREE RITUALS

SHARLYN HIDALGO

Llewellyn Publications
Woodbury, Minnesota

FIRST EDITION
First Printing, 2019

Book format by Samantha Penn
Cover design by Kevin R. Brown
Cover illustration by Meraylah Allwood
Editing by Annie Burdick
Interior Tree illustrations by Meraylah Allwood
Wheel of the Year Diagram by Llewellyn Art Department

Llewellyn Publications is a registered trademark of Llewellyn Worldwide Ltd.

Library of Congress Cataloging-in-Publication Data
Names: Hidalgo, Sharlyn, author.
Title: Celtic tree rituals : ceremonies for the thirteen moon months and a
    day / by Sharlyn Hidalgo.
Description: First Edition. | Woodbury : Llewellyn Worldwide, Ltd., 2019. |
    Includes bibliographical references.
Identifiers: LCCN 2019012525 (print) | LCCN 2019019203 (ebook) | ISBN
    9780738760803 (ebook) | ISBN 9780738760223 (alk. paper)
Subjects: LCSH: Magic, Celtic. | Tree worship. | Ogham alphabet. | Ritual. |
    Rites and ceremonies. | Religious calendars.
Classification: LCC BF1593 (ebook) | LCC BF1593 .H53 2019 (print) | DDC
    133.4/3--dc23
LC record available at https://lccn.loc.gov/2019012525

Llewellyn Publications
A Division of Llewellyn Worldwide Ltd.
2143 Wooddale Drive
Woodbury, MN 55125-2989
www.llewellyn.com

Printed in the United States of America

Other Books by Sharlyn Hidalgo

The Healing Power of Trees
Celtic Tree Oracle

I dedicate this book to the trees and to nature. Mother Earth provides us with a paradise to live upon and it is my dream that we respect her and protect her. The trees have been my teachers and I am grateful to the ancient teachings that come out of the lands that my ancestors hail from. My journey to discover early spiritual teachings from the British Isles has provided my life with rich meaning. I find that offering ceremonies that carry me through the Wheel of the Year enriches my relationship with Source—and keeps me close to the seasonal changes through the years, and my own personal changes. I am so very grateful for this incredible gift of life.

CONTENTS

ACKNOWLEDGMENTS

I would like to thank all the teachers that have shared their knowledge with me and supported me since I was a young woman. I have special love for all of my students through the years. I am grateful to my friends and family for having my back. I honor Source and the magic of the realms, seen and unseen, that makes up the tapestry of my life. I treasure the learning: all the invaluable information that I have gleaned from astrology, the tarot, energetic healing systems, the Egyptian Mysteries, and the British Mysteries. Lastly, I acknowledge the incredible journey it has been to learn as much as I have, and to have the opportunity to share that learning in this book—this is what dreams are made of. I am ever grateful to Llewellyn and to you, the reader.

INTRODUCTION

This book offers you magic, healing, and spiritual teaching from the trees. The tree rituals that you will find here have come out of my own practice, developed through years of work with the wisdom of the Celtic tree ogham and the Celtic tree calendar—they keep me close to nature. I have found that the calendar (which is composed of a portion of the alphabet) provides a meaningful doorway into the Celtic cosmology. It is a powerful body of wisdom and teaching for today's seekers. Many goddess worshippers, Neopagans, Wiccans, tree lovers, and native European spiritualists have based their spiritual practice upon these teachings. I hope it can be useful to you the reader.

The Tree Ogham

The tree ogham (oh-am, ohm) is a medieval alphabet of twenty-five sigils/letters/trees that we can still find on stone monuments throughout the British Isles today. The alphabet consists of a set of straight lines that were etched upon sticks called staves, or on stones, and used for markers or monuments. Each line forms a sigil and can be written vertically (usually read from bottom to top) or horizontally (usually read from left to right). The markings are made along a stem line called the druim.

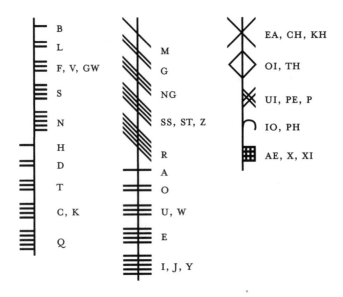

The alphabet was not used for writing or speech as we know it; it was mainly used for mundane and practical communications. However, it is likely that it was also used to indicate ideas and beliefs related to the more ancient Celtic cosmology and philosophy.

The Celtic Tree Calendar

The Celtic tree calendar is a modern adaptation and is based on the concept that the letters in the ancient Celtic ogham alphabet corresponded to a tree, and that each of these trees is associated with the themes of the ancient Celtic culture and mythology. This calendar is used as a time-keeping device for moving through what modern Pagans call "the Wheel of the Year," celebrating the holidays and using ritual and ceremony to honor the healing energies of the tree portals known as the tree months. Each tree month has its own special teachings, totems, guides, and deities.

There are two versions of the calendar. One is solar and begins just after the Winter Solstice and has a slightly different order: Beth, Luis,

Nuin, and so on. The other is lunar and begins on November 1, the Celtic New Year, and ends on October 31, Samhain. This follows the order Beth, Luis, Fearn, and so on, and it is the one I choose to work with.

The Celtic tree calendar that I use is a lunar calendar consisting of thirteen twenty-eight-day months plus a day—amounting to 365 days in total. It is made up of the first fifteen ogham of the twenty-five-ogham tree alphabet (two trees are shared to fit into the thirteen months) plus ogham twenty-one, which represents the extra day. Thus, the calendar consists of fifteen phonetic consonant sounds and covers all the days of the year up to October 30. October 31 has its own special phonetic sounds and ogham, number twenty-one: the Koad/Grove/the Day. The calendar provides a powerful framework for spiritual practice with the trees through the thirteen moon months of the year and a day—and I have written rituals, ceremonies, and stories out of my experiences with it.

The Gifts of the Calendar

The gifts of Celtic symbolism and mythology—which come through in the tree teachings of the calendar—with their profound connection to the natural world and to the mysteries, have fostered in me a deeper connection to nature and have provided important and meaningful guidance. So, by following the teachings of the trees and the Celtic wisdom within this form, the calendar has proven to be the foundation of my practice.

By following the monthly sequence of the tree teachings, I have come to be a better steward of the planet and a more conscious human. This tree lore from the British Isles connects me to my ancestors and to their wisdom. This powerful teaching from the ancients can help us to survive today and encourage us to take care of our planet. I am ever grateful. I believe that this information is sourced in the ancient knowledge that was passed on orally and lost to us—and yet has reawakened like the phoenix. It is my hope that the calendar will be useful to you for your own spiritual growth and enjoyment.

How to Use this Book

The Celtic tree calendar is based on thirteen moon months and begins the new year on November 1 with the Birch tree and ends on October 31 with the Grove. I like to begin my year with a ceremony on November 1 with this first lunation cycle. If this is where you choose to start, it may be useful to begin your study and focus on the portal of Birch, which runs from November 1 to November 28. Otherwise you can find the appropriate month that you want to focus on. I like to begin a month and use the whole time for learning about the tree and its teaching, then culminate the time spent by inviting a few friends to share a ceremony. You can also modify the ceremonies to do them solo. It's also wonderful to choose a ceremony to honor the celebration of each of the eight holiday sabbats, which I have included in this book.

The phenomenal healing power I have witnessed in the teachings of the trees—which shows up for folks in ceremony, meditation, and journeying—has left me in awe time after time. Divinity cannot be found in dogma. It shows up through the magical, the mystical, and the unexplained, and it is simply beautiful. It is to be experienced. All we need to do is extend the invitation, open to the energy, and make some time, whether this be individually or with a group.

We can also communicate with our ancestors and our loved ones that have passed over and receive the loving support and guidance of the totems, guides, and deities in the unseen world. This is our birthright, and the Celts understood that this communication is meant to help us to live well and live in harmony with all life on our planet. I have found this to be true. Thank you for opening yourself up to the tree teachings and their healing power. This spiritual practice, which moves you through the cyclical changes of the seasons and the years, will surely enhance your life.

Please take note that some of the totems, guides, and deities that I have included are modern additions to the teachings and that from time to time I use other mystery school totems, guides, and deities. They became part of my practice when I opened myself up to the energies of the ceremonies through the years. Egyptian, Norse, Native American,

Greek/Roman, and other influences have shown up. To me they just add richness to the medicine that we are creating. I hope that I will not ruffle any feathers for not sticking strictly to the Celtic mythology and knowledge. When I talk about a deity from another culture, I will show a parenthetical notation alongside and share where it comes from. If it is bothersome to you, the reader, simply substitute a Celtic totem, guide, or deity that you are familiar with.

As for the stories, I wanted to share with the reader my real life experiences with the unseen help offered by the trees—the tree spirits themselves, as well as the totems, guides, and deities that show up. I also wanted to demonstrate the truth—that the ancestors and our loved ones who have passed on are alive and well, albeit in other dimensions, and will act on our behalf if we just ask. Indeed, the veil between the worlds *is* thin. I want to share ways that you can invite these healing relationships into your life. You'll find these methods at the end of each story.

It is my work with the trees that brought me to these experiences and enriched my life. The energies and healing teachings of the trees will also communicate with you if you but ask and offer them your interest and attention. The more time you spend communicating with them, the better the relationship you establish. As such, you create a better connection for receiving their wisdom, healing, and magic.

I invite you to trust your dreams, intuitions, yearnings, synchronicities and serendipity, visions, daydreams, and inner guidance. Listen for that quiet voice within. Take note of books, movies, people, and events that attract you. These can act as guideposts along the way. Use meditation, guided journeying, and creativity as well, as a means of connecting you to Source wisdom. Create art, write poems and prose, keep a journal, write songs, play music, move, sing—allow the creative spirit to dance through you. Pay attention to body symptoms. Ask specific symptoms for their messages.

The tree spirits and their wisdom and knowledge are accessible. Ask the totems, guides, and deities for their help. Guidance and support is offered. They offer us healing. We do live in a paradise of beauty, mystery, and magic, and there are doorways between the worlds built to ensure communication. This communication can strengthen character, lead you through dark places, and support you to be a better steward of our Mother Earth. This pathway can help you with creativity and community. You can create a daily walk with peace and joy and gratitude.

How to Create a Tree Ceremony

Welcome and Greetings

Welcome your participants to your ceremony and thank them for taking the time to join with you in sacred ritual. Begin with greetings and introductions and state the purpose of the ceremony. Pass the talking stick and have each person say their name and why they came to the circle. Take a moment for silence and have your participants close their eyes and breathe together. Ask them to leave their daily concerns behind as they enter sacred space.

The Talking Stick

Choose a special stick to use in your ceremonies. You can decorate it with shells and colored ribbon if you so desire. Alternately, respectfully gather a stick of the tree that you will be honoring in each ceremony.

Share the rules of the talking stick. The holder of the stick has the floor for however long they need it to express themselves. There is no cross talk while someone is holding the stick. If someone needs clarification or has a comment to add, they must ask the holder of the stick if they might do so. There is no need for the speaker to say yes to this. The speaker can respond with "No, not at this time." There is an agreement that no one talks about another's story outside of the circle without permission. They agree to hold this circle as sacred and private.

Call in the Directions

Call in the directions and invite the guides, totems, deities of the tree, and the tree dryad. When you are done calling in the directions, stand together. Visualize a forest of trees. Tone together as you feel the power of the Grove.

Here is an example that you might use for calling in the directions. Simply read it out loud. After you are comfortable with calling the directions you can write up your own or simply wing it.

"I call the East, the rising sun, and springtime. I call new beginnings and new ideas. I call the Winged Ones. I call a higher perspective to all our endeavors. I call the element of air, and I honor the four winds. I honor intelligence, inspiration, and communication. I honor the trees of the East and their deities, totems, guides, and guardians.

"I call the South, the midday sun, and summer. I call fertility and creativity, passion and activity. I call the plants, flowers, and trees. I call the element of fire and honor our passions, sexuality, and desires. I honor purpose and will, action and creative endeavor. I honor the trees of the South and their deities, totems, guides, and guardians.

"I call the West, the setting sun, and autumn. I call the dreamtime and inner reflection. I call all water creatures. I call the element of water, and I honor all the waters of the earth. I honor our tears, emotions, and feelings. I honor flow and receptivity. I honor the trees of the West and their deities, totems, guide, and guardians.

"I call the North, the midnight sun, and winter. I call the wisdom of the ancestors and the knowledge of our lineages. I call the element of earth, and I honor our bodies that house our spirits. I honor the rocks, minerals, crystals, gems, mountains, valleys, prairies, fields, and deserts. I honor two-legged and four-legged animals and all the creepy crawlers. I honor the trees of the North and their deities, totems, guides, and guardians.

"I call Above. I call the star nations, higher dimensions of consciousness and love. I call the gods, goddesses, and the angelic realm that participate one hundred percent in love and protection for all. Welcome to our circle.

"I call Below. I call Mother Earth and give great gratitude for all she does to sustain our lives. I give great gratitude for all creatures and the unseen domain that nourished us. Without her permission, there would be no flora or fauna to sustain us. She is a paradise and it is a privilege to walk upon her.

"I call Within. I honor our heart's altar, and I feed the flame of love. From this inner place we receive everything we need to know. This is the home of our own inner world tree and our knowledge and love. The heart is the true master organ, where our true eyes and ears live. This is our master message center that connects us to all that is: past, present, and future. This is the place outside time and space, and the emptiness within which all potential and possibility rest. And so it is!"

Teachings

Teach about the meaning of the month. Your intention is always to open to the portal of the tree to receive its teaching and guidance, or to celebrate one of the eight high/holy days of the Wheel of the Year. State the intention for the celebration. Examples could be inspiration, healing, connecting with the ancestors, or giving gratitude.

Sing

Pass out papers with song lyrics. I suggest that you buy a few of the CDs listed in the appendix so that you can make your own list of songs. You can also go to the internet for women's circle songs or Pagan songs. I also recommend recordings from these performers: Jennifer Berezan, Susan Osborn, Jami Sieber, Holly Near, Cris Williamson, Libby Roderick, Charlie Murphy, Rhiannon, and Feron. Once you are familiar with some songs, make copies for your participants. In appendix II, I have mentioned songs that will fit well into the ceremony themes.

Introduce the drum as the connection to Mother Earth. She is the heartbeat of Mother Earth. Practice drumming together and teach songs or play CDs or tapes if you are too shy to sing. Music is always a wonderful addition to ceremony. I have also written chants that you may use, or you may create your own.

Chant

The chants included are meant to be read out loud by the leader. These can be repeated many times to build up the energy.

Read

These sections are an indication that the leader of the ceremony is to read the text out loud for the group.

Guided Meditation

Take a guided journey. You may create your own guided journey or use the sample journeys I have included here. Always set the mood by asking your participants to close their eyes and go within. Allow them some time to pay attention to their breath and let go of their daily concerns. Allow them time to be with the silence before you lead them through the journey. Then read the meditation provided out loud. Allow them time at the end of their journey to come back and ground and center before moving on to sharing. The unconscious can use the imaginal realm to provide information, guidance, and healing. Thus, what is offered spontaneously within a guided journey can provide amazing results.

Sharing

Make time for your participants to share. Giving them time to write their experiences in their journals helps them to remember better. Journeys are like dreams; the details can fade quickly.

Activities

Here you might plant seeds or draw or do any number of other exercises. Choose something that grounds the teachings. Recommended activities are provided in each ceremony, but feel free to experiment with your own connected ideas.

The Celtic Tree Calendar

1. Beith (beh) / Birch: Nov. 1–Nov. 28 / Beginnings / Snake, Phoenix, Eagle / B: ⊢

Celtic New Year: Nov. 1

2. Luis (loo-ish) / Rowan: Nov. 29–Dec. 26 / Protection / Horse, Chiron / L: ⊨

Winter Solstice: Dec. 21/22

3. Fearn (fair-un) / Alder: Dec. 27–Jan. 23 / Guidance/ Raven, Wren, Dragon / F, V, GW: ⊨

4. Saille (sahl'yeh) / Willow: Jan. 24–Feb. 20 / Feminine Principle / Bee, Dove / S: ☰

Imbolc (immol'g): Feb. 1

5. Nuin (nee-an) / Ash: Feb. 21–Mar. 20 / World Tree, So Above, So Below / Dolphin, Hanged Man / N: ☰

6. Huathe (hoh'uh) / Hawthorn: Mar. 21–Apr. 17 / Cleansing / Fairies, White Stag / H: ⊣

Spring Equinox: Mar. 20/21

7. Duir (dur) / Oak: Apr. 18–May 15 / Strength / Bull / D: ⊣

Beltane (b'yol-tinna): May 1

8. Tinne (tinn-yeh, chin-yuh) / Holly: May 16–June 12 / Justice, Bringing Opposites Together / Swan, The Lovers Card / T: ⊣

9. Coll (cull) / Hazel: June 13–July 10 / Intuition, Wisdom, Higher Perspective / Scarab, Turtle, Crab, Salmon / C, K: ☰

Summer Solstice: June 20/21

10. Quert (kyert) / Apple (shares the month with Hazel): Choices, Beauty / Fairies, Mother Goddesses, Gaia, Ancestors / Q, CC: ☰

11. Muin (muhn) / Vine: July 11–Aug. 7 / Prophecy / Lion / M: ⟍

Lammas, Lughnasadh, Lughnassad, Lughnasa (loo-na-sa): Aug. 1

12. Gort (gor'it) / Ivy: Aug. 8–Sept. 4 / Labyrinth into Inner Knowing / Spider, Wolf / G: ⟍

13. Ngetal (nyettle, ing-tal) / Reed: Sept. 5–Oct. 2 / Direct Action, Becoming a Hollow Reed / Owl, Pike / NG: ⍦

Fall Equinox: Sept. 21/22

14. Straif (stryf) / Blackthorn (shares the month with Reed): Negation, Learning from Challenges, Renewal / Crone Goddesses, Grim Reaper, Scapegoat, Death and Devil Cards / Ss, St, Z: ⍦

15. Ruis (roosh, roo-ish) / Elder: Oct. 3–Oct. 30 / Renewal / Cranes, Storks, Ibis / R: ⍦

16. The Koad / The Grove / The Day, Oct. 31: the Temple, the Silence, the Void, Initiation, Meditation, Recommitment to the spiritual path, Communication with the ancestors and loved ones who have passed on / Personal Guides and Guardians / Vowel and consonant combinations / Ea, Ch, K: ✕

Samhain (sow-in): Oct. 31

Ending

End with gratitude for your tree dryads and all the spirit helpers. Release the directions by saying: "We release the Center, Above, and Below; the North, the West, the South, and the East with our gratitude. Thank you for blessing our ceremony. The circle is now open."

The dark half of the year begins officially on Samhain or October 31 and was given special attention in the Celtic cosmology. It marks a time to communicate with the ancestors and to reconnect with one's spiritual path. The Celtic New Year begins on November 1. The light half of the year begins on Beltane or May 1.

There are four winter trees that span the Winter Solstice: the Birch, the Rowan (which rules the Winter Solstice), the Alder, and the Willow (which rules Imbolc). This north quadrant in the Wheel of the Year represents the earth, winter, and the Pentacles in the tarot.

There are three spring trees that span the Spring Equinox: the Ash, the Hawthorn (which rules the Spring Equinox), and the Oak (which rules Beltane). The east quadrant represents the air, spring, and the Swords in the tarot.

There are four summer trees that span the Summer Solstice: the Holly, the Hazel and the Apple (which share a month and rule the Summer Solstice), and the Vine (which rules Lammas). The south quadrant represents fire, summer, and the Wands in the tarot.

There are three fall trees that span the Fall Equinox: Ivy, Reed, and Blackthorn (the latter two share a month and rule the Fall Equinox). The west quadrant represents water, fall, and the Cups of the tarot.

The final thirteenth tree month is ruled by Elder. The Elder is a corridor month and represents your uniquely personal magical tools and your personal allies.

The Trees Around the Wheel of the Year

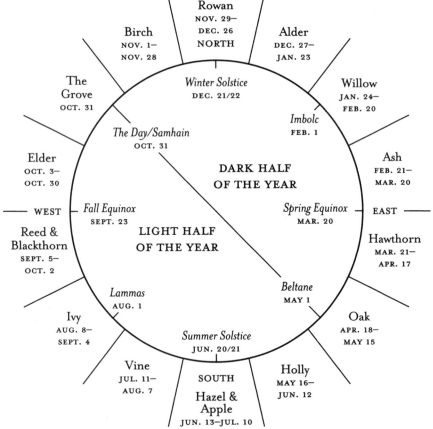

The last day of the year is October 31 and is its own special day. It is ruled by the Grove. It can be celebrated as The Day or as Samhain. This is a time to renew spiritual commitments and honor the ancestors.

The Sabbats/Holy Holidays

There are four lunar holidays or cross-quarter celebrations and four solar holidays within the modern Pagan Celtic Wheel of the Year. As you move through the calendar chapters, you will find ceremonies for the holidays at the end of the tree month that they fall in. Thus, some of the months have two ceremonies: one for the honored tree and one for the holiday. Please check the dates of the solstices and equinoxes each year, as they fluctuate.

As we move through the Wheel of the Year and encounter the teachings of each tree, we also work with totems and guides and with god and goddess energies. These are central to the themes of death and rebirth. The ancient people of the British Isles all honored the Triple Goddess in her many forms and names and she is embedded in their stories and mythology. The Goddess represents the feminine initiations through life, the lunar cycles, and Gaia's seasonal changes. Today in Pagan traditions it is common to refer to her as mother, maiden, and crone. The Goddess retreats in winter to the underworld to join the crone, emerges as the maiden in the spring, and becomes the mother by summer, only to retreat again in the fall.

The White Stag, Herne the Hunter, Cernunnos the Great Stag God, and the Green Man are found in Britain's folklore. Today in Pagan traditions, this quaternity reflects the special relationship between man and animals and the masculine path of initiation into the mysteries. The story emphasizes man's responsibility as the protector of nature and symbolizes his willingness to sacrifice himself for the good of his people.

We celebrate the Green Man at the Winter Solstice and thank him for protecting the deer family. At the Spring Equinox, the Stag emerges from the forest, and by the Summer Solstice the hunter comes to search for the Stag who will renew his divine power. At Lammas, the hunter mates with the representative of the great Goddess, the deer goddess

Ker. By the end of summer, the Stag is killed and his horns are placed upon the hunter who becomes Cernunnos, the Stag God. He reigns through the fall, but by the Winter Solstice he must return the horns and the power back to the earth. Like the grains and the corn, the antlers are returned to the earth as compost. The hunter returns to the woods to become the Green Man once again. He becomes the protector of the spirit of the wild animal.

But foremost, it is the Goddess in her many forms that blesses and participates in this cycle with the masculine. She empowers it, and thus ensures the regeneration of life through the seasons. She is the creator and the Great Mother and central to the cosmology.

The Holidays

October 31	Samhain: Halloween, Hallowmas / Falls within the Grove / The Day
November 1	The Celtic New Year: Nos Galan Gaeaf / Falls within the Birch month
December 21–22	Winter Solstice: Alban Arthuan, Midwinter, Yule / Falls within the Rowan month
February 1	Imbolc: Imbolg, Candlemas, Brigantia / Falls within the Willow month
March 20–21	Vernal Equinox: Alban Eiler, Easter, Eostre, Ostara / Falls within the Hawthorn month
May 1	Beltane: Beltain, May Day / Falls within the Oak month
June 20–21	Summer Solstice: Alban Heruin, Litha, Midsummer / Falls within the Hazel and Apple month
August 1	Lammas: Festival of the Bread, Lughnasa, Lughnassad / Falls within the Vine month
September 21–22	Autumnal Equinox: Alban Elved, Mabon, the Harvest / Falls within the Reed and Blackthorn month

How the Unseen Realm Communicates with Us: A Story about Dragons, the Totem of Alder

Totem helpers, guides, and deities, as well as the spirits of the trees and plants, can come through dreams, synchronicity and serendipity, visions, daydreams, and guided meditation. They can also show up through art, spontaneous writing, dance, body symptoms, and unusual and unexplainable experiences. They can appear in your waking life and send you messages through inner dimensions. Sometimes you will want to connect with a healer to help you sort out the messages you receive. When you work with these guardians and helpers, you will begin to see actual results in your daily life. I share this story with you to demonstrate this reality and how it played out in my life.

Dreams

Spirit helpers can come through dreams. They often come at times of stress or challenge, but sometimes they appear out of the blue. My initial involvement with dragon medicine came some thirty some years ago with a particularly lucid dream.

I was beginning to learn how to read the tarot and I dreamt that large tarot cards were sitting on the water in the large strait called Saratoga Passage that lies between what was once my father's beach home on Whidbey Island and the opposing Camano Island in Washington State. This is one of my most favorite places on earth. These cards were very large and reminded me of the playing cards that became the bodies of the Queen and King of Hearts and their guards in the Disney movie *Alice in Wonderland*.

In the dream, the tarot cards were lying face down on the water. They began to ripple with the movement of the currents until they sat upright and arranged themselves in a row to form the undulating back of a huge water dragon. I could see her spikes roll and peak as she moved, and I was amazed at what I was watching. I was sitting in our little row boat. As the dragon became more lively and fierce, I began to feel afraid. I started to row for shore, and the dragon began to chase me.

When I got to shore, my husband helped me pull the little boat up onto the sand. I was fully expecting him, whom I considered my knight, to defend me. Instead he thought we should pull the dinghy over on top of us and hide. I didn't have time to show my surprise because the dragon was almost there. We pulled the boat over us, hull-side up, and waited to see if the dragon would attack. She snorted, and a huge bolt of fire issued from her mouth. She pushed the boat aggressively with her huge snout. She was determined. I hoped my husband would try to defend us, but he was frozen.

It was up to me. I darted out from under the boat and jumped to my feet. In my hands I carried a double-edged ax, the kind that belongs to the Amazonian women fighters. As the dragon came forward I swung backward, and with all my might and determination, I swung the ax over my head and pulled down. I met the flesh of the mighty dragon at her neck. Her head fell at my feet. The huge body of the sea serpent dropped to the side with a loud, dead thump. As amazed as I was, I placed my foot upon her flank and claimed my victory. I had saved us!

I awoke from that dream very surprised. I was filled with power. I was the dragon slayer, but I was disappointed by the man in my dream. He was supposed to have defended me and saved me. It's a shame I didn't understand the guidance of the dream. No man could have fulfilled my need for him to be the perfect white knight. If he had tried I would have fought him tooth and nail. The truth was I didn't need a protector and would never find my own power while I was looking to someone else for approval. It just took a long time for me to come to this truth.

In hindsight it was too bad I didn't celebrate my own power then, but instead chose to keep it asleep and hidden. I wanted something from this man that he could never give to me: my own sense of self. Too bad I spent so long trying to get him to change. Too bad I spent so long being angry and frustrated and distraught. What a waste of life energy ...

It took me a long time to put my attention on my own quest. It must have been a level of emotional development that I needed to grow through; it was just easier to blame others and I didn't know any better at the time.

The dream had given me a blueprint for myself and I am sorry I didn't see my first encounter with the sea serpent as an honoring and blessing. The dragon of the tarot, with all her archetypal secrets, had chosen to show herself to *me*! And I had responded with fear and suspicion. I was not mature enough at that time to understand her gifts. I had killed her and chosen to go back to sleep. However, it is impossible to kill important messengers from the unconscious, especially when they are intertwined with one's destiny. She did not give up on me.

Art

Surprising images can come through our artistic creations. It is a direct line of communication from our Source and our inner life. The purpose is to bring healing and understanding to guide and support us.

The next year, my husband and I moved to Alaska to teach school. It was in a remote Native American village that I painted my first dragon. I felt like I needed protection and I spontaneously painted a green dragon on a shield on my canvas.

This was a very intuitive act. There was a wild death in this place. Between the Baptist minister who thought that the dragon was a sign of Satan, the teachers who were doing their fair share of drugs and alcohol, and the Native people that told their own stories of killing witches, I felt threatened. So much alcoholism and drug use by the villagers as well as the white teachers, and so much suicide among the young Native people made me sad. Even the gigantic ravens spoke in unison of stark defeat and threat. Too much taboo, too much loss, too much conflict between Christianity and Native religion, and too much fear...

The dragon got me through. This is when I began to reconsider the meaning of my original dragon dream. There might have been another message, or I began to have a hint that I could have responded differently in my original dream.

We returned home to Seattle when I became pregnant with my son. During my pregnancy I painted a huge painting with a castle in the center, and all around it I placed symbols of fertility and fecundity, as well as a raven. At one side was a dragon's tail, although I did not really understand that is what I was painting. I had always thought of it as a strange shape at the edge of the painting. The dragon seemed to live behind the scenes as I prepared to become a mother and a keeper of the hearth. This was in 1981.

Dragon didn't awaken again until 2003 at a women's workshop with my friend Starfeather. By this time much change had come into my life. I was divorced, remarried, and had another child. I created a mandala using collage and found the most wonderful, colorful dragon to place upon it. It was then that I was reminded that the shape in my painting was exactly the shape of this dragon's tail. I created the mandala with the dragon's tail on the right side and the head of the dragon appearing on the left side, with the idea that her great, powerful body was wrapping back behind the shield unseen. It was as if dragon had woken up and shown herself. I found this wonderfully pleasing. Perhaps she knew that I was ready now to welcome her into my life. She was patient, as it had only taken me twenty-two years to remember her! So here it was, so many years later and my dragon had returned.

It was as if once I recognized the dragon again through my art she made herself known. She came a few months later in my dreamtime in full force. I was asleep and she flew into my room with a huge whoosh of sound and air. Huge, green, and vibrant, she hovered above me and then transformed into a hooded cobra. This was a very strange dream indeed! The cobra entered my body and at that moment I was infused with the kundalini energy of dragon and cobra. It felt like a tremendous spiritual initiation, and again this felt real, very lucid. Was it a dream at all?

Body Symptoms and the Need for Helpers

Therapists, naturopaths, acupuncturists, and healers can become part of our healing team, and I encourage this. For many months after this experience I began to suffer incredible heat in my digestive tract. Sometimes we just have no idea what is happening to us and we need to get outside help. I finally went to an acupuncturist and he placed a needle into the place on my belly that was extremely tender. So much heat came out of the site that we both burst into sweat. It was like an erupting volcano. We were very surprised—astounded. After that I began to heal.

I went to another healer after this who suggested that we dialogue with what she sensed was my inner dragon. Through this dialogue, I discovered that my dragon had not realized that her natural heat was making me sick. Yet she did not want to come out of me because she thought I lacked the fire and fortitude to do the work she wanted me to do.

The healer also sensed that there was a knight inside who was fighting with the dragon because he believed she was evil and that his job was to slay her. He was acting as my protector. I invited both to come out of my body and I asked them if they would agree to work with me. Their job of course was to protect the realm and ensure that I would have the muster to fulfill my destiny. They agreed to help me restore balance. We also agreed to work as a team to help others, as this was the dragon's greatest desire. She was there to help me with my mission and my destiny.

Unfortunately, I had also developed frozen shoulder during this time. My body was so uncomfortable. I began to receive two-hour massages to heal my shoulder pain, and during one of those sessions I went into a trance. Within the session I experienced the birthing of a baby dragon from my shoulder. In my mind's eye this little fledgling was wet and new, and her wings did not open yet. I began to move and stretch my shoulders and arms, as if I was the newly born dragon. My arm became unstuck and I began to unfurl my wings. There was a healing that day. I was unfrozen! And it felt like a miracle!

Attention Is Your Coin

Attention is your entrance fee into the unseen realm. The more attention you give to your totem, the better the relationship you build. You can do this by setting an intention to meet up with your totem, before you dream or before meditation. You can draw and paint your totem.

You can learn all you can about your totem through books and classes. You can dialogue with your totem in your journal. You can write up your own guided journeys and record them. Join with others and lead them on a guided meditation to meet their totem helpers.

Synchronicity

When things start coinciding straight out of the blue, you know you are on the right track. When things come together in surprising ways that get your attention, you can bet that your helpers and guides are wanting to communicate with you.

At a used bookstore, I found some books on sale about the Celtic mysteries and the Celtic tree calendar. When I got home I began to read a section on dragons. Then the mail came and in a large manila envelope sent from my friend Maxine was a beautiful colored picture of a maiden and her dragon. It was the same exact picture of a dragon that I had chosen for my collage when I was at Starfeather's workshop! Synchronicity! I felt that this set of synchronicities was encouraging me on with my work with the trees. And my dragon guide seemed pleased.

To this day, in January every year, I love to honor the Alder tree and her totem, the amazing dragon. As such, the dragon has become an important guide for me. Dragon is of the earth and represents the ancients. I deeply appreciate her persistence, guidance, and protection. From my ancestry and my dreams and my own experience, I have come to know the dragon. Now I court my own dragon guide and call on her. The dragon was most gracious not to abandon me for my early immaturity. I hope to keep strengthening my connection to the dragon and to dragon medicine.

I have been drawing more and more dragons and studying them as time goes on; I feel they are my friends. In another guided meditation, one became small and sat in my lap and purred! To me, the dragon is a great protector—she helps me to stay in touch with my own ancestral heritage. She carries the elemental power of the earth herself. She also represents the element of spirit and creative fire. For the Chinese, she is good luck. She is a symbol of impersonal power, wild and free, yet she is willing to guard and protect you. She is a symbol for vigilance and will safeguard your possessions, your home, and your life. She helps to keep me on track and reminds me to continue to open to all that I can be.

I am happy to have dragon as a helping totem. She comes from the unseen world of what may have once been. She offers teaching and guidance. Although she lives in other realms she offers herself. She only needs to be asked. Perhaps dragon has information for us that could be helpful for our survival as a species. Perhaps dragons know how to help with this because they have lived since the beginning of time.

I just feel the dragons urge me forward. They say, "keep writing, keep teaching, keep listening, and keep knowing that you are one with all." They say, "keep believing in magic and enchantment and involve yourself in the very mystery of your true nature."

Go back through your own recurring dreams and look for totem helpers that have shown up through the years. Look at synchronicities. Check out the art you are attracted to and the movies or song lyrics that you like. Are there recurring totems that show up? What about body symptoms? What messages have you received?

We know that these are ways that our unconscious—our inner life—communicates with us, as well as the larger cosmos and spiritual realms that we are a part of. We each have our own guardian angel and our own set of helpers. They will answer if you ask. They cannot help us without our permission. They will show up for you if you want to meet them. There are workshops for finding your totem. Or you can get together with friends and lead a guided meditation for finding your helpers. As you move through the ceremonies you will also be led through the meditations to meet some of the totems, guides, and deities as well as the dryads of the trees. It is like getting new friends and adding them to your family. They will enrich your life!

BEiTH-BiRCH

November 1—November 28
First Lunation, November

Ogham: Beth, Beith (beh), B: ⊢

Keywords: Endings and new beginnings, death and rebirth, cleansing and purification, releasing old patterns, overcoming difficulties, pliability, reestablishing boundaries, renewal, shedding unhelpful influences, resolution of conflict, returning to innocence and seeing with new eyes, letting go of judgment

Totems: Snake, phoenix (Greek), eagle, and falcon

Guides and Deities: The crone aspect of the Goddess; the mother, crone, and cauldron-keeper Cerridwen; the Cailleach; the hag; the medicine woman

Practical Guidance: Begin again. Make a new start. Clean up your clutter. Make amends and let go.

Beith/Birch Month Ceremony

Holiday

The Celtic New Year is November 1.

Purpose

To honor the portal of Birch. To let go of the old and begin a new cycle of life.

Preparation

Buy some apples, leaving one whole to cut in the ceremony, and gather seeds from the others so you have enough for your participants to plant.

Welcome and Greetings

Welcome to our Birch month ceremony. Introduce yourself and go around the circle, having each participant share their name and why they came to the circle. Have them close their eyes and share a moment of silence to prepare for the ceremony.

Call the Directions

Call in Birch tree energy (beginnings) and the totems, guides, and deities of Birch (snake, phoenix, eagle, and falcon). Call in the Crone Goddesses that we honor at this darkening time of year. Call in the Celtic New Year and set the intention of letting go of that which is no longer needed as you open to the new. Take a moment to consider new dreams and possibilities.

Teachings

Share about the themes of the Birch month: beginnings and endings; elimination and regeneration; letting go; reinvestment in your own spiritual truth; resolution of conflict; giving thanks for your own pliancy in recovery after a trauma; weeding out thoughts, feelings, and actions that impede your own growth; returning to innocence; giving up judgments and prescribed expectations; letting in magic. Release the need to judge, compare, and analyze; in other words, give the left brain a rest. Seek a higher vision.

Sing

Choose songs that have to do with fall or the beginning of winter. Any song that honors the Goddess is appropriate.

Chant

> What is the teaching of the Birch? Let go.
> Our freedom comes from not holding on.
> Behold! We die and the crone births us again.
> And we are free to create our new year.
> We seek a higher vision.
> What is the teaching of the Birch? New beginnings.

Guided Meditation

Close your eyes and focus on your breath. Allow yourself to slow down and let go of your daily concerns. Allow yourself to rest easy and relax. Follow each breath. Be in this quiet place for a few moments.

Imagine yourself standing within a grove of lovely Birch trees. It is November, so you are bundled up and cozy within your warm cloak or coat. Notice the slender white bark of these trees and their whispering leaves as the branches dance with the cold wind. Allow yourself a moment to close your eyes and see, sense, feel, know, or imagine this moment of stillness, accept the whisper of the moving leaves and branches of these trees.

In this very moment, you shape-shift, and you magically find yourself becoming a slender Birch tree. You have entered this tree and now have an opportunity to communicate with the dryad of this tree family. Take a moment to feel this experience ... (pause)

Notice your graceful branches as they reach up toward the light and then gently bend down with the weight of your many heart-shaped leaves that rustle in the wind. Notice your pliant yet strong white and silver trunk, and your root system that extends down deep into Mother Earth ... (pause)

As you experience the stance of this tree and its special way of moving and being, give it your gratitude. In the silence of this November day, feel the grace of this tree. Feel its energy move up toward the light. Listen to the whispering leaves. They have a message for you ...

Think of this tree's ability to shed its skin. Allow yourself to drop habits and ways of thinking that are limiting in the same way. See your old "bark" simply blowing away. As an eagle flies to the very top of your tree, allow yourself to see with the eyes of the eagle. View your problems and concerns from a higher perspective. What can you learn from your situation? What can you forgive in yourself and others? What stubbornness, grudges, resentments, or need for revenge can you let go of? What judgments about yourself or others no longer serve you? Simply let go, let go, let go ...

Allow your participants to sit quietly and reflectively in the dark while you play some soft, uplifting music.

Take a moment to give your gratitude to the spirit of Birch.

Sharing

Call your participants back into the room. When everyone has returned from their journey, have each person share something from their experience. They may have revelations to share about letting go of judgments. They may have an intention of seeing things in new ways without negativity.

Activity: Planting Apple Seeds

Next, we honor the powerful crone energy of this portal. Have each participant share the names of their mother and grandmothers and elders as a means of paying them homage. Example: "I honor my mother, Marjorie, my maternal grandmother, Hannah, my paternal grandmother, Jane, and my maternal great-grandmother, Clare, and her sisters, Maude and Ruth." After all the names have been called forth have your group give gratitude to the ancestors and the energy of the elders, crones, and female lineages.

Cut an apple through the middle and pass it around so that everyone can contemplate the symbol of the pentacle. Say: "Just like the seeds form a pentacle in the center, so is there a pattern of perfection for each person within themselves."

Then pass out apple seeds to each person and ask them to plant their seed within a pot of soil at the center of your altar. As they plant their seed have them speak out loud their intentions for the Celtic New Year.

Ending

Give gratitude to the Birch tree for its teachings. Take a moment to stand like trees, feel rooted in the earth, with arms spread outward to the skies. Tone together. Have them notice how the group carries the energy of the grove. Have them place their hands upon their hearts and connect with and experience their own inner knowing so that they may walk the month and the new year in a good way. Release the directions and all the helpers and guides and open the circle.

A Birch Story: A Higher Perspective and Healing

Three white Birch trees stand proud and strong right across the street from where I sit and write. I see them through my large picture window every day as I sit down to write from my dining room table. They are slender and graceful. They reach tall and as they sway and rustle in the wind, their bending limbs and bountiful leaves remind me of ballet dancers. In fall they look like fire with leaves of gold and red. In winter, depleted of their leaves, their branches bend and struggle with the storms. In spring, their delicate green leaves dance with the breezes.

I am reminded of their help in disputes as I view them today. They add reconciliation and peace in times of disruption and distress. I took Birch energy from these three trees with me to a circle I attended whose members were in turmoil over our differences. I remembered that one of the teachings of this tree is to drop judgments and preconceived ideas about what will happen. I dropped my fears and agenda. Birch offered me the presence of mind to consider that there is always the possibility of a miracle. When we don't know but we show up, there is room for what seems impossible. Magic can appear. I cleared my mind and set my intention for the highest possible outcome for all involved. I resolved to trust the process and call in the power of the Birch. I was amazed that my group moved from terrible distrust, agitation, and fear to a peaceful and graceful resolution. I learned a lot about the grace of Birch that day!

I watch these trees through the seasons. Now in fall, some of their bark unravels and their leaves of gold fall onto the grass below. They look like golden flames against the sky. Last winter when there was an incredible ice storm, the trees were frozen in a thick transparent covering of ice. The limbs of each tree drooped with the weight of the ice, and on one of the smallest trees, a branch leaned way out from the tree and looked like it would break. We all held our breath, but the branch never broke, even as it moved closer and closer to the earth. As the ice melted, the branches of each tree returned to their original position, showing their pliancy and ability to recover. The only branch that remained dangerously low and out of position was the one smaller branch. My family all feared the tree would lose that branch. We watched it all winter and spring, but it wasn't until summer that the traumatized branch regained its symmetry to the tree. The branch held the memory of pliancy in its healing, but it took its own sweet time. What a lovely lesson about the process of any recovery.

The whiteness of these Birch trees is so fresh, their upward stance so lovely. I am reminded of the endings and beginnings of this every year. This new year could not start well until the old one had been finished and the unwanted and unhealthy influences sent back into the ethers for their own higher transformation. Birch helps me to leave the confusion of the tangled and thick underbrush of my own overthinking, to look up, out, and beyond for clarity. I remember the open sky and the expansiveness of the air above. I can reach up for the light. I can count on Eagle to provide me that higher overview as she lands on Birch's highest branch.

Allow yourself the time you need. Let go of that which is imped-
ing your progress. Allow the eagle to show you a larger perspective, a
higher view. Forgive if you can. Forgive yourself. Birch offers you a new
beginning. She encourages you to turn the page and begin your story
from this fresh new perspective. It is a new year, it is a new day. Every
change comes from a decision made each moment. Birch encourages
you to take the higher road. She offers you regeneration and clarity.

How can you apply her teaching? How does the Birch's story of taking her time to heal apply to you? What does she teach about patience
and endurance? Is there a controversy or difficulty that you are experiencing that you can apply her wisdom to?

LUIS–ROWAN

November 29–December 26
Second Lunation, December

Ogham: Luis (loo-ish), L: ⊨

Keywords: Protection against enchantment or the control of others, discrimination, astral travel, connection to ecstasy, universal unconditional love, higher consciousness, connection to the mystery

Totems: Horse, centaur, and the wounded healer Chiron (Greek)

Guides and Deities: Horse goddesses like Epona, Macha, and Rhiannon

Practical Guidance: Spiritual protection is offered to you. Trust in this.

Luis/Rowan Month Ceremony

Holiday
The Winter Solstice is December 21/22.

Purpose
To celebrate the Rowan tree portal and embrace the mystery. To encourage us to bring our light to our planet and to receive healing.

Preparation

You will need a cauldron or bowl of dirt for your altar with a large central candle and enough smaller candles for each of your participants.

Welcome and Greetings

Welcome to our Rowan month ceremony. Introduce yourself and go around the circle having each participant share their name and why they came to the circle. Have them close their eyes and share a moment of silence to prepare for the ceremony.

Call the Directions

Call in the Rowan energies (protection, ecstasy, astral travel, the mystery) and her totems (horse, centaur, and Chiron). Invite in the Great Mother. She represents all mothers who give birth and manifest the miracle of the creation of life within the womb. Call Mother Mary, Isis (Egypt), Kuan Yin (China), or any other goddess you are comfortable with as representative of the divine feminine principle. Call all the mothers of the avatars that have helped enlighten the planet. We invite winter and the wisdom of nature and the ancients who listened carefully to what nature had to say. We call in the midnight sun and the darkness. We call in the quiet and the deep silence of winter. We honor hibernation and the resting seeds and bulbs below the ground. We lastly call in the spirit of the Rowan that represents the mystery. We honor the cycle represented by maiden, mother, and crone.

Teachings

The Rowan tree and her totems are all about entering and experiencing the mystery. This is a time to celebrate ecstasy and astral travel. Rowan offers protection when you travel in other dimensions. She can connect you to unconditional love and higher consciousness. She is all about bliss. Honor the Priestess of Rowan in the form of the Welsh goddess as Rhiannon or Modron. They are shape-shifters, and when they are honored they will work with you in amazing ways. Also recognize the mother in the form of the mare/mother Epona, and the crone in the form of Cerridwen.

Sing

You may choose your own songs. I suggest using the internet to find women's circle songs. Choose songs that go with the theme of the mystery and connecting with the ancestors.

Chant

> *What is the teaching of the Rowan? Ecstasy.*
> *Our bliss comes from a flight on our spirit horse to the stars.*
> *Behold! It is our birthright to journey within the healing*
> *mystery of the universe.*
> *And we are blissful knowing that we are*
> *protected and loved as we travel in this way.*
> *We seek higher consciousness.*
> *What is the teaching of the Rowan? Unconditional love.*

Guided Meditation

Turn off the lights and sit in the darkness. Choose to play some music that reflects the mystery or choose any music that puts you in a dreamy space.

Ground and center and breathe into your heart. Pull the energy from the earth up into your heart and breathe it out in all directions. Pull the energy from above through your crown chakra and into your heart and breathe it out in all directions. Take a few moments to experience this breath… This is an adaptation of the heart breath that I learned from my teacher, Nicki Scully.

Take a couple of deep breaths and imagine yourself walking along a path in a snowy landscape. The sun is out and the snow crystals twinkle at you. The view is beautiful, serene, and ever so quiet. The earth is covered in a blanket of snow. You are glad that you are dressed so warmly.

Ahead of you is a grove of Rowan trees. You notice this beautiful grove of Rowan. You see that the landscape is filled with beautiful Rowan trees, still holding on stubbornly to their clusters of red or orange berries. They welcome you as you follow the path that leads to them.

You remember that each berry holds the sign of the pentacle at its center, the symbol for Mother Earth. As you breathe in the scent of this forest, you find that there is inspiration offered to you in this place of all possibilities. You have entered the dimension of the Priestess of Rowan. Stop for a moment to notice the sacred vibration that exists here in this magical place.

You are aware that a beautiful priestess begins to approach you. She wears a crimson cape with a hood fringed with feathers, fur, and jewels. She comes and places a crown of Rowan leaves and berries on your head. Look deeply into her eyes and see the love she has for you.

She invites you to tell her what your soul yearns for. Tell her what your dreams are. Tell her now how you would like to bring light to the planet. When you seek her protection and guidance she will become a staunch ally for you. Take some time to receive her offerings … (long pause)

Show her places in your body, mind, or soul that are distressing you. She will gladly lighten your load, give you inspiration, renew your enthusiasm, and make you laugh. She will heal you. Feel the grand possibility of all miracles.

She asks you if you are willing to enlarge your belief system to include more and more of the mystery and magic of creation as you connect to these higher dimensions of love. If you are, nod your head. With this final exchange, she enfolds you in a healing embrace. Look at her, eye to eye, and thank the Priestess of Rowan for her presence in the world and for her attention and love. Begin to ground and center in this place and in this time. Stay here quietly for a moment and ponder the beauty of your experience.

Upon returning, write your experiences in your journal. Do this to ground your experiences, because, like dreams, the details are easy to forget if you wait too long to record them.

Sharing

Allow time to share the experiences of the participants on their journey.

Activity: Candle Lighting

Light a central candle within a cauldron of earth to celebrate the returning of the light. Invite each person to light a candle and share how they would like to bring more light to the planet. Then each person states something they require healing for.

Ending

In closing, thank the directions and the center. Place the names of people or situations in the center for healing. Remember that you can return to the Priestess of Rowan and to the grove anytime you like. Rowan offers protection and will connect you to miracles and the mystery. Give your gratitude and release the directions. Say, "The circle is open."

A Rowan Story: Mystery and Magic Close to Home

When I began my tree studies, I would seek out each tree in the Celtic tree calendar and sit with it—draw it, gather its leaves and branches, and intuit its teachings. But when it came to Rowan, I didn't know what one looked like. I looked the tree up in the library and in my encyclopedia (before the days of the internet), so I had a general idea of what I was looking for. I looked as I walked and as I drove, but I just couldn't seem to find one. I had a clear picture of the distinct leaf pattern and the little red or orange berries with the pentacle at the puckered end. I was on the hunt, but I was frustrated. I looked and looked without success.

One day I was in the backyard wondering where I was going to find a Rowan tree. I then noticed a tree that had leaves and berries just like Rowan. Then it hit me! Here was a Rowan, right in my own backyard! This was such a lesson. One can look far and wide, but what one seeks can only be found close to home. That home is within!

Over time, the little tree in my yard shared much with me. I have had lots of talks with my Rowan. But usually she reminds me that the answers are within myself. She invites me to become quiet and meditate. The magic of finding her in my yard was so delightful and so unexpected. She has indeed charmed me and encouraged me to believe in miracles and to include the mysterious and magical in everything I do. She reminds me that astral travel is possible not only in my dreams, but when I take the time to meditate or go within.

In meditation I picture my Rowan tree and I always hail the horse of my astral travels, and the centaur Chiron. My horse is available to take me anywhere I would like to travel. And Chiron reminds me that my body is holy. He is forever providing me wisdom through my body if I just listen. If you have a bothersome body symptom, ask him for advice and information. Often when we heed the messages, the symptoms disappear. The berries of the Rowan with their little pentacles of protection remind me that it is a blessing to be in a body upon this planet.

I give great thanks for winter, for the wisdom of my body, for the wisdom of the ancients, and for the teachings of Gaia and her trees. I am ever grateful to the little Rowan tree that was right in my own backyard.

Check out the trees in your backyard and in your neighborhood. Sit with them. Talk with them. Build relationships with them through your time and attention. Collect their leaves and berries and seeds and branches that fall to the ground. (You never really have to cut these from the tree.) It is polite to ask for permission when you take them from the ground around or near the tree. Then give your gratitude.

See if you can locate a Rowan tree to make friends with. Visit your chosen trees often. And then in your quiet time, revisit them in meditation. Invite in their totems, guides, and deities; you may be surprised. They will work with you to enrich your life. When you receive messages or images it is great to write these in your journal, write a poem or song, or paint a picture to ground in your experience.

Winter Solstice Ceremony
December 21/22

In the Northern Hemisphere, we celebrate the Winter Solstice and the beginning of winter toward the end of December. The solstice marks the shortest day of the year and the longest night. This holiday represents the rebirth of the goddess/god and the return of the sun—the light and the promise of spring returning. Another name is Yule.

Purpose

To celebrate the Winter Solstice. To increase our light into the world.

Preparation

Prepare the affirmation on page 40 with enough copies for your group. Also prepare simple affirmations on long, thin strips of paper. Ideas: You are loved. You are cherished. Your dreams are coming true. Success is already yours.

You will need a cauldron or bowl of dirt for your altar with a large central candle and enough smaller candles for each of your participants.

Welcome and Greetings

Welcome to our Winter Solstice ceremony. Introduce yourself and go around the circle having each participant share their name and why they came to the circle. Have them close their eyes and share a moment of silence to prepare for the ceremony.

Call the Directions

We give our gratitude to our Mother
Earth, to nighttime, and to winter.
We honor the darkness because
this is where all gestation begins.
We ask that the wisdom of this
portal support the journey of our days.

We love the earth and the sun
and the moon and the stars.
We give our gratitude to the
Great Spirit that leads us.
As we embrace the silence and we
appreciate the sacredness of our lives.
And so it is.

Teachings

The theme is rebirth. The divine birth giver is the Crone Goddess. She personifies the midwife-priestess. We too act as midwives to welcome the rebirth of the sun. We also honor the birth and return of the special sons and teachers born to holy women. This is the longest night of the year and so we honor the darkness. We keep the Yule log burning, seeking the fire of hope in the winter of the life of the year. We celebrate the promise of new life ahead. Themes for this time of year are:

• Honoring the parts of ourselves that are dying
• Transmutation: the eating and drinking of the gods and goddesses, ingesting their power
• Endings: change and transition, transformation
• New beginnings
• Rebirth, renewal, resurrection
• Turning the Wheel of the Year

Sing

Choose songs that call back in the light. This is a time of the birth of the sun and we honor the many sons that were said to be born at this time. We give gratitude that the sun enlivens our lives and brings new beginnings every year.

Chant

What is the teaching of the Winter Solstice?
Life begins within the darkness.
We die and are reborn in this darkest hour.
Behold! The crone beckons the light's return.
Transformation comes from endings and rebirth.
What is the teaching of the Winter Solstice?
The promise of new life.

Guided Meditation

Take a moment to go within and close your eyes. Listen to your breathing and focus on your heart. Slow down and be with the darkness here. Enter the chamber of your heart. Find a place to sit upon the floor within the chamber of your heart. This is a dark and safe place for you. You are held. You are loved. Be here in this quiet safe place. This is your very own sanctuary. Here you are mothered by Gaia herself. As you are a child of the earth, she knows you. You are one of her dear children. Within this space, be willing to set down your burdens and concerns. Let them evaporate into the acceptance that is here. Allow yourself to nestle into safety. Allow yourself to be held.

Being within this dark, safe spot is like returning to the womb. You are a seed and you are meant to grow into your full magnificence. You are reminded that you begin here but you are a light being with a purpose. At the least, your purpose is to share your light. Take your time here. Let the dark embrace you and fill you with unconditional love.

You notice light streaming from beneath a closed door and you stand and move toward it. As you do so you give your gratitude to the dark from which all things manifest. You are happy to have spent some sacred time with this fruitful darkness at the center of your own heart. You feel restored and renewed.

You open the door easily and walk through into the daylight. You see that the sun is rising. You feel the promise of the returning light on this new day and the days that will lead you forth toward more sunlight. For although you have passed through the darkest night of the year, you have been comforted by the dark. You know that a whole new cycle of life begins here in the dark.

You may have a sense of renewal. New ideas and new projects may come to mind. You may sense a deep desire that you wish to manifest. You may bring seeds of ideas and wishes and desires back with you from this meditation that will spur your creativity for new endeavors. Trust this. This is the beginning of the new. Take a moment to review your time within the sacred darkness. And then as you look at the rising sun, think about your new plans. Remember that you too are the light, that the sun and you are one. You are meant to shine your own light out into the world.

It is time to return to our ceremony. Give your gratitude and slowly come back. Be gentle and take your time. You can return to this safe place within your heart anytime you choose. When you are ready, open your eyes…

Affirmation

Prepare this affirmation beforehand with enough copies for your group. The group reads together:

> Tonight, we each have an opportunity
> to increase the light within our world.
> And yet here we stand within the darkness of winter.
> The paradox is that it is within the darkness that
> we find the beginnings of new life and light.
> And so, as the darkness nourishes us and hold us
> Let's invite the coming light to bring in new
> horizons of possibility.
> And let us welcome these possibilities to
> grow within ourselves and our world.
> Let us share and affirm our personal wishes
> for an increase in the light of our world.
> And so it is.

Activity: Bringing the Light into the World

Say: "Reflect for a moment on how you would like to bring light into the world. What are you hoping for? What do you want to create? What light do you want to see more of? How can you increase the light that you already share?"

Have each member light their individual candle from the light at the center and plant their candle in the bowl of earth as they speak. Have them express what they would like to create. How would they like to bring greater light into the world?

Read

> The light is beckoning us. We are waiting for its return as we share here for a moment together in the darkness and silence of winter. At the solstice, we give our gratitude for both. We give our thanks for the turning of the wheel of the seasons. This celebration is the time to sit in the silence, reflect, and listen. Can you hear the songs of the cosmos? Can you hear the music of the earth, the sun, and the stars? Can you hear the melody of the flora and the fauna of our planet? Can you hear your own heartbeat? Let us rejoice in this mystery of life and light returning, that is the great holy miracle of this season. Let us too honor her darkness as well, for it is here that the mystery of life is born. And so, as the earth spins, turning from dark to light, may we celebrate the music in our hearts and the dancing of our jubilations. May we give our gratitude that we are part of the great mystery.

Sing

Choose a song that calls in the light.

Activity: Affirmations

Have each participant choose an affirmation from a bowl at the center and read it out loud.

Sing

Choose an ending song that has to do with keeping the light alive. Or simply choose from these ending songs: "May the Circle Be Open," "Merry Meet," or "We Are a Circle."

Ending

Give gratitude for the teachings of the solstice and release the directions. Say: "Here ends the solstice mystery." Open the circle.

FEARN–ALDER

December 27–January 23
Third Lunation, January

Ogham: Fearn (fair-un), F, V: ≣

Keywords: Guidance, oracular power, prophecy, help with decisions, spiritual protection, stability, strong foundations, balancing of male and female aspects

Totems: Wrens, ravens, blackbirds, crows, kingfishers, dragons

Guides and Deities: Welsh—Bran and Branwen, the Morrigan

Practical Guidance: Build a strong foundation for your goals.

Fearn/Alder Month Ceremony

Holiday
The Solar New Year is January 1.

Purpose
To honor the portal of the Alder. To receive guidance and get into touch with the power of the oracle. To make an Alder wand and participate in

an empowerment exercise so that it can be used as a tool for guidance, protection, and balance.

Preparation

Have your participants bring a six- to twelve-inch stick or a small branch of an Alder tree that they find on the ground, so that they can begin to build the energy for creating their own tree wand. Have some ready that you have found, in case some in your group can't locate an Alder. Choose and print some pictures of Alder from the internet.

Welcome and Greetings

Welcome to the Alder month ceremony. Introduce yourself and go around the circle having each participant share their name and why they came to the circle. Have them close their eyes and share a moment of silence to prepare for the ceremony.

Call the Directions

Invite the energies of Alder (guidance) and her totems, guides, and deities (raven, wren, and dragon). Have leaves, berries, and tassels of Alder upon your altar so that your participants can touch them and directly contact the spirit of Alder. Have a bowl of water there to honor Alder's affinity with water and emotion. Give gratitude for the protective energies of the Alder.

Teachings

The Alder provides protection and strength in any difficulties or challenges that we may face in this new solar year ahead. Alder also brings balance between our male and female inner aspects. Alder will provide guidance as well as prophecy, if but asked.

Give thanks for Alder's ability to bring nutrients to the soil. Ask your participants to close their eyes for just a moment and envision this tree in front of them. (Some may not know what an Alder looks like, so have some pictures of Alder on the altar.) Have them invite in the power of this tree and see this tree transmitting nutrients to their whole being. It is like receiving a megadose of vitamins, minerals, and invigorating energies. Have them open their eyes and continue.

Ask your participants to contemplate a question they have that they will be able to ask the Priestess of Alder. This may have to do with any difficulties, blockages, physical concerns, or future desires and goals. Give them a few moments of silence to do this ...

Chant

> What is the teaching of the Alder? Balance.
> She offers us strength as we meet our challenges.
> Behold! She offers us protection and guidance.
> She is our wise oracle.
> We seek her council.
> What is the teaching of the Alder? Trust.

Guided Meditation

Close your eyes and go within. Simply follow your breath. Allow yourself some time to sit in this quiet space. Allow yourself to become quiet as you pay attention to your breath. Take your time with this ...

I invite you to travel internally to a grove of Alder trees. The trees sway with the wind and offer you welcome. Alder is especially helpful in guidance, prophecy, or protection. The Alder grove is sacred and there is a strong, potent healing force here. First be willing to feel the protection all around you. Alder is here to ensure your safety. Simply allow this strength to encircle you. Let the energy know what you especially need strength and protection for right now in your life ... (pause)

The Priestess of Alder approaches you. She wears a soft green, floor-length cloak and around her neck is a pendant that boasts the picture of a dragon. Her eyes are green and her red hair is long and flowing, blown gently back off her shoulders by the wind. She is most willing to be consulted as you seek guidance. She looks into your eyes and asks you what your concern or question is ... Be willing to ask your question and receive your answer, as she is the oracle. She draws a tarot card for you from her cloak pocket and shows it to you. Take a moment to see the card and its symbols. Listen to her message for you ... (long pause)

When she is complete with her message she asks you to tell her what your favorite oracle is. Take a moment to contemplate this. Is it the runes, the tarot, astrology, the *I Ching*, the tree cards, the ogham, or others I have not mentioned? After you have let her know, she touches you at your third eye and blesses you in her own ancient language. You feel the transmission. The only thing she asks of you is to spend some time with your favorite oracle or to see someone you trust who can read for you. Through your chosen oracle she will come to chat with you and share more of her wisdom.

It is time to give gratitude to the Alder grove for its protection. Give gratitude to the priestess. The priestess takes your hand and holds it to her heart and you feel her love. Again, give your heart-filled gratitude. It is time to return to this time and this place. Ground and center and when you are ready, you may open your eyes.

Sharing

It is always a good idea to write your journey down afterward to help ground it and to keep it fresh in your memory. Have the group share their experiences. They may remember their question or concern and the tarot card that the priestess shared with them. What oracle did they choose?

Activity: Reading the Tarot Cards

Place your tarot card deck out facedown and have each participant choose a card as they seek vision for the next year ahead. Go around the circle and have each one read their own card just as they see it and apply it to their question or situation. Remind them that they have all the intuition they need to read their own card.

Activity: Empowering the Wands

Today we will create a tool of power. Have your group stand and ask them to point their wood stick toward the center.

Read

> By the power of this new solar year, your wand is empowered.
> By the power of this third lunation, your wand is empowered.
> By the power of the Priestess of Alder, and her totem the
> raven, that connects you to spirit, your wand is empowered.
> By the power of the trees, your wand is fully yours to be
> used for bringing guidance, protection, and balance into the
> world!
> And so it is!

Pause, then say:

> And with these words your wand has become a tool of
> power for you. You can take it out and listen to its guidance
> when you are having trouble making decisions. You can ask
> for its prophecy and await its messages. You can carry it with
> you when you require protection or stability, or feel out of
> balance. She can help you to build strong foundations.

Sharing

Encourage your participants to take their newly empowered wands home
and beautify them with paint, beads, and other embellishments. Then
have each person talk about the stick they chose to bring to circle and
how they would like to use it as their personal wand of power.

Sing

Choose an ending song that has to do with empowerment or one that
unites the circle. Or choose from "May the Circle Be Open," "Merry
Meet," or "We Are a Circle."

Ending

State that healing is offered in this sacred space or cauldron that has
been created by this sacred circle. Ask your participants to go around

the circle and place people, situations, and events in the center that require healing. Give your gratitude to Alder and her totems, deities, and
guides and release the directions. Open the circle.

An Alder Story: A Lesson in Permission

Many years ago, I had two young Alders growing up along my drive
way, probably seeded from the large old cluster of Alders across the
street. They were beginning to become quite tall, and I noticed that
they would be growing straight into the electrical and phone wires that
ran from the telephone pole to my home. I figured it would be easy to
simply pull them out at this early stage in their growth and save myself
the hassle of later having to cut them or trim them constantly. This happened before I started to study the trees and their energies.

I went to pull the trees out, but the first one would not come out easily. So I got my trusty little saw and cut its slender little trunk very close
to the ground. I decided to wait to cut the second tree until the next
day. I cut a small piece from one of the branches of the cut tree so that I
could create a wand for my full moon ceremonies.

That very day I was at the library getting books for my young daughter and with a little extra time on my hands, I looked up the Alder tree
in the section on Celtic spirituality. I read that it was very bad luck to cut
an Alder, or to take a twig or a branch from an Alder for a wand! Oh, I
was surprised to read this on the very day I had cut the tree for a wand.
There were those synchronicities again!

The next day, I went to the second little Alder tree and asked for forgiveness for my lack of information and understanding. I put my hand
on the small little bare stump and asked pardon. I told the standing tree
that I would protect it and not cut it down. I touched it with a newly
formed gratitude and respect. The row of large Alders across the street
began to move and sway. I felt their rustling and experienced this as
their acknowledgment of my newly found understanding.

I asked for permission to create a wand from the branch I had taken
and immediately felt that this would be okay. I gave my gratitude and
I committed my wand to the memory of the Alder I had cut down.

I offered to teach others about the trees and to protect them. The tree let me know that there are many times when branches and twigs are offered, naturally, without the need to cut, and that they were glad to have me on their team.

As I write this piece, I have my little wand right here. I know it is time to finally carve and decorate this wand with a crystal. In further study, I have come to believe that the "bad luck" idea came from the ancient understanding that this tree appears to bleed when cut. It also was known for its fierce fighting energy. I now believe that the tree can be approached with respect and that when it is honored it will give permission to take a branch for a wand. Respect for its strong female and male nature and its tie to the oracle and guidance ensure its permission. I am also reminded that what we need is often provided by the natural loss of twigs and branches, and that we can find these on the ground close to the tree. I have never taken anything from a tree again without forethought and permission. Alder taught me a great lesson that day.

Look around your neighborhood and see if you can find an Alder tree. Go on a search. Find a branch that you can fashion into your own wand. You can probably find one on the ground. Ask the tree for permission to take the branch.

You can cut it to six inches or so and strip the outer bark. Then you can oil it or paint it and add colored thread or ribbon to which you can tie bells and shells and other ornamentation. Find a lovely crystal of your choice that you can fix to the end of your wand. Take time to understand the teachings of Alder: guidance, balance of your male and female aspects, oracular power and divination, and protection. When you are experiencing a challenge, keep her close as she can act as a "bridge over troubled waters." Begin to build a relationship with this powerful new ceremonial implement. It is your tool for supporting a dialogue between the worlds, and a healing flow of guidance and protection through the portal of Alder.

SAiLLE–WiLLOW

January 24–February 20
Fourth Lunation, February

Ogham: Saille (sahl yeh), S: ䷀

Keywords: The feminine principle, cooperation, fertility, intuition, the moon and her cycles, water, emotion, creativity, community, shared power, women's issues and themes

Totems: Bee, dove

Guides and Deities: Brigid/Brigit, the maiden aspect of the Goddess

Practical Guidance: Listen to your dreams, intuition, and imagination. Create.

Saille/Willow Month Ceremony

Holiday
Imbolc is February 1.

Purpose

To celebrate the portal of the Willow and honor Brigid. To focus on healing, creativity, and our power to manifest through our intentions.

Preparation

Make copies of the principles of manifestation from appendix A and your personal tree of manifestation (included here at the end of the ceremony). Have colored pens or pencils available.

Greetings and Welcome

Welcome to the Willow month ceremony. Introduce yourself and go around the circle having each participant share their name and why they came to the circle. Have them close their eyes and share a moment of silence to prepare for the ceremony. You can use a Willow branch for a talking stick.

Call the Directions

Call in Willow tree energy (the feminine principle, creativity, cooperation, healing of the feminine) and the totems, guides, and deities of Willow (bee and dove). Call in the energy of Brigid, the maiden aspect of the Goddess, with her love of creativity and inspiration. Have the participants call in the divine feminine in the names they are comfortable with, aloud or silently.

Teachings

Share about the Willow tree for the month of February. Willow represents lunar rhythms; the bleeding cycle and the blood mysteries; "night vision," better known as our intuitive giftedness; and the female collective. Willow helps us to manifest our heart's desires. She is the muse for all creative acts. She is our inspiration. The celebration of Imbolc/Candlemas and Brigid/Brigit falls within the Willow month. The Goddess Brigid represents the crescent moon phase of beginnings. She is the spark and beginning of the growing seed beneath the ground. We honor the magic of that seed igniting into growth after the winter's rest. We too are ignited with this magic as our deepest heartfelt desires and wishes begin to grow. Brigid is all about creativity and inspiration. The dove and the bees as the totems of Willow represent our ability to work together in community. We are encouraged to create sweetness like the bees and peace like the dove in everything that we create together.

Sing

Sing songs and drum together. Choose songs that honor women, the earth, and the trees. We especially honor the maiden aspect of the Goddess.

Chant

> *What is the teaching of the Willow? Peace.*
> *Our sweetness comes from sharing.*
> *Behold! The magic spark of life returns.*
> *And we are happy to build community.*
> *We seek inspiration from the feminine.*
> *What is the teaching of the Willow? Create beauty.*

Sing

Choose songs that honor the maiden aspect of the Goddess. Remember you can always play music for your group if you are not comfortable singing. On the other hand, drumming and creating songs or chants on your own is great fun.

Guided Meditation

Sit quietly and take some deep breaths. Go to your heart center and breathe into this place. Allow all that has transpired in your day to fall away. Simply become your breath and feed your heart flame. Watch it grow and allow that warmth to spread out to every part of your body.

Let your busy mind quiet through the softness of your breath and the quiet of the room. Take some time with this...

Imagine yourself in a meadow. Just in the distance you see the most magnificent Willow tree. Notice her long, slender leaves and the way her branches bend to the ground. Her trunk is strong and sturdy although it is hard to even see her trunk through her amazing foliage. She is large, and her expansive branches provide a huge umbrella of protection from wind, storm, or too much sun. She is nurturing and present to you. Feel her beckon you to her.

Move toward her and duck under her leaves and branches to go to her trunk and touch her. Does she respond back? Take a moment to feel this communication... Thank her for her majesty. Acknowledge the breath she provides you. Look up and see the sky through her branches. Look down and see the magnitude of her root system. In your mind's eye, find a comfortable place at the base of this tree where you can sit as you journey with Willow. Sit with her energy for a time. Rest here in her healing presence. (Long pause)

Now you feel a beckoning coming from beyond the tree. Give your gratitude to your Willow tree, and as you walk out from beneath her umbrella of leaves, see a figure walking toward you. She is Brigid. Take a moment to see how she comes to you. Notice what she is wearing and what she looks like as she comes right up and greets you with her youthful smile. (Pause)

Brigid holds the secrets of the feminine principle. She is the keeper of the moon and lunar rhythms and all cyclical patterns. She holds the magic of fertility and procreation and she holds the secrets of the blood mysteries. She upholds the dignity of the feminine and she understands the incredible magic of giving birth, whether it be a child or a creative pursuit or project. She protects, nurtures, and mothers. She knows your pain and she is aware of the long history on our planet of assailing the feminine principle. She knows what we seek healing for.

She represents the blessing of intuition and emotion. She loves all the water of the planet, be it the rivers, streams, lakes, oceans, the rain, or your tears. She has much to teach about cooperation rather than competition. She offers us a positive image of female fertility and power and the collective. She is the spark of creativity and she is the muse for all creative endeavors.

Look at Brigid eye to eye and give her your gratitude. Take a moment to embrace the gifts of Brigid and honor her feminine light. Are you willing to perceive yourself as a woman or man in this same sacred light? Are you willing to promise this goddess and her tree, the Willow, that you will always treat them, as well as yourself, with esteem? Let them know. (Pause)

As you stand with Brigid, listen and sense, or simply imagine and come into communication with her. She has courage and energy to share with you. Let her offer her healing energy to you. Listen to her message. (Long pause)

She wants you to embrace your own creativity and she encourages you to contemplate the power of your ability to manifest. Brigid reminds you of the magic of that spark that ignites all beginnings. She wants you to listen to your own inner voice and your nighttime dreams. She encourages you to go deep and take seriously your heartfelt desires. She invites you to write poems, listen to music, and do creative things. She asks you to use your tools of divination. Listen and receive from her. What does she say to you about what you truly desire? (Pause)

She says that these are the times when the creative spirit of humans and nature can work together for healing on the planet and it will come from the people when they stand up together and know they are powerful creators of their own lives. She says that you are sacred; she says that she is sacred. From that sacred knowing you can transform your world and it starts with you. Spend a few minutes with Brigid talking about what it is you wish to create. (Pause) She sends you her bees to remind you to make honey, and she sends you her dove to remind you to create peace.

Stay with your Brigid for a few minutes and thank her for her many gifts. Promise her that you will honor her and that you will honor yourself. When you have finished it is time to say goodbye. Stand firmly in your own feminine light (whether you are a man or woman) and honor the place in the cycle of life that you are. If you are a man, honor the women in your life and your own feminine side.

Sharing

Very gently, come back to this time and this space. You can return to this Willow and to Brigid anytime you like, because they live inside of you. Pass the Willow branch around and share a brief account of the journeys.

Activity: Manifestation

In the spirit of Brigid's encouragement, pass out copies of the principles of manifestation (Appendix A of this book) and go through them.

State: "It is important to know that your desire is already yours, and to give gratitude as if you have already received your manifestation. It is important to feel the emotion of receiving. Thought, word, and emotion are important. Intention is everything."

Make copies of page 59 or recreate the page yourself, giving each person a paper that has these words written at the top: "Your Personal Willow Tree of Manifestation: I am grateful for and gladly receive my good. I am so grateful for already receiving my heart's desire, which is…"

The bottom half of the paper should have a large circle drawn upon it. Have colored pens or pencils available.

Ask them to draw a Willow tree within the circle as best they can without any judgment about being an artist. And then have them write on the paper a desire they want to bring into manifestation. Have them take a moment to really experience the feelings of already having what they desire and then feeling the emotion of wonder and gratitude.

Then go around and have everyone share their drawing and their desires. When finished going around the circle, each person should use their image of this tree to hold and support that which they choose to create.

Stand together, holding your papers to your hearts.

Read

> Together we invite our tree helper and Brigid to infuse this work with their powerful and supportive energy. We are creating together. We are manifesting together. We are healing together. We are witnessing the sacred. We are witnessing together the healing power of trees. We are calling forth the creative power of Brigid in all her bright wisdom and creativity. We call forth the peace of the dove and the able cooperation of the bee that knows how to work within community for the good of all. We are transforming the world through our heartfelt dreams and desires. And for the highest good of all, we manifest this or better. If it harms none, so be it. Blessed be.

Sing

Choose ending songs that embrace the maiden aspect of the Goddess or choose "May the Circle Be Open," "Merry Meet," or "We Are a Circle."

Chant

> *She is the crescent moon. She is our own lovely daughter.*
> *She is the seed of our creativity. She lights the candle at Imbolc.*
> *She is our inspiration. She is our beloved Goddess Brigid.*

Ending

Thank the seen and unseen helpers, Brigid, the spirit energy of the Willow tree, the bees, and the dove. Give thanks to each participant for their participation. In closing, ask each participant to look at trees as sacred, to take the time to slow down and feel the trees' energies, to develop a dialogue with them, and to understand their immense love and life-giving benefits for their human companions. Release the directions and open the circle.

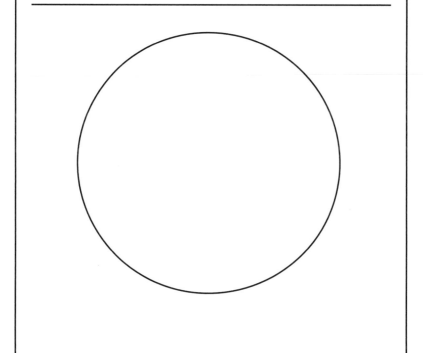

Your Personal Tree of Manifestation

I am grateful for and gladly receive my good. I am so grateful for already receiving my heart's desire, which is ...

A Willow Story: Give the Universe a Little Time

In February of 2003 I was preparing a workshop I was to do for the Women of Wisdom Conference in Seattle. This was a wonderful yearly conference that lasted a week and brought in famous female spiritual leaders as well as local presenters to teach about women's spirituality. My workshop was entitled The Healing Power of Trees and I was focusing on Willow tree energy.

Weeks before the conference I began searching for a Willow tree, but I just couldn't find one. As the days passed I was still unable to locate a Willow. Finally, on the day before the workshop, as I was driving home from work, I remembered one of the principles of manifestation that I had learned. If what you are doing isn't working, try its opposite. "Oh, stop looking!" I thought to myself, "I'll just give the universe a little time to consider my need."

Then, right on the next block, lo and behold, I spied a gigantic Willow tree. "Wow!" I thought to myself. I stopped the car, got out, and asked the tree if I might have a few of her branches to use in my ceremony. She allowed this. And then as I looked down the street I saw another Willow. As I gathered some branches I noticed how long, graceful, and supple they were. I took a moment to contemplate what it means to be graceful, supple, and flexible. I gave my gratitude.

I used one of the branches in my workshop as our talking stick, and some thirty-five women held her power in their hands. She provided her gentle healing to all of us as we placed the remaining branches at the center of our altar in a beautiful vase.

I kept these branches in water at my home for quite some time afterward, and I watched them bud and sprout forth in the spring. Willow has never been the same for me since inviting her energy in to help teach about the healing power of trees. Whenever I see Willow I feel blessed and am reminded to honor the feminine principle and my own female light. She is such an incredible healing force. Now I find Willow trees everywhere!

When you begin to work with a specific kind of tree you will open to new teaching and new experiences. See if you can find a Willow tree to build a relationship with. Spend time with this tree. Gather her branches and leaves and pods. Although she is an incredible healer for any distresses and challenges that relate to women, she also offers healing for our grief and loss. Here is list of themes that this lovely tree will assist you with:

- Loneliness and depression
- Grief caused by change
- Grief after losing a loved one or a pet
- Abandonment, separation, or divorce
- Menstrual challenges
- Miscarriage, death of a child, abortion, or giving up a child for adoption
- Grief of not being able to have a child
- Issues of abuse and violence
- Injustice

There is so much to be healed under the umbrella of Willow's protection. If you are suffering with one of these issues, sit with Willow and ask for her healing. She is a balm for our pain. You can breathe in her mothering unconditional love and protection. She also directs us to work in groups or to create support circles. She reminds us that connection with others is another important aspect of healing and moving through our pain, trauma, and isolation.

She also is a muse. What are you excited to create? The energy of this tree and her guide Brigid will infuse you with inspiration and enthusiasm if you but ask. Make a list of what you want to create with colored pencils and invite in the energy of Willow to support you to bring these into manifestation. Place your list on your mirror or close at hand. Review the principles of manifestation and use them regularly. Above all, remember that your attention is your coin, your payment for entrance into this work with the spirits of the trees. The more time you spend with the energy of Willow, the more she will offer you.

Imbolc Ceremony
February 1

Imbolc is the first of the cross-quarter moon celebrations, falling six weeks between the Winter Solstice and the Spring Equinox. This is a fire festival that celebrates the return of the sun. Lighting candles and hearth fires or bonfires brings light and warmth into the darkness and cold and represents the spark of new life that is sprouting within the seeds buried beneath the soil. Imbolc is represented by the crescent moon and the maiden aspect of the Goddess, especially the creative goddess Brigid or Brigit. We are renewing our own sacred fire within. This is a time of year for initiations, recommitment to your spiritual path, and new plans for creative and artistic ventures, as well as your new ideas and enterprises, goals, and aspirations.

Purpose

To celebrate Imbolc—or Imbolg, Candlemas, Brigantia.

Preparations

Fill a little cloth bag with small spiritual objects like feathers, clay ornaments of the Goddess, a piece of wood, shells, beads, a miniature statue, or other interesting things. This will be used for oracle readings. Prepare the "I am a powerful and wise person" reading on page 69 so that everyone has a copy.

Welcome and Greetings

Welcome to our Imbolc ceremony. Introduce yourself and go around the circle having each participant share their name and why they came to the circle. Have them close their eyes and share a moment of silence to prepare for the ceremony.

Call the Directions

> We are the East and the air. We are the growing light. We are the seed bursting forth. We are the thinkers full of innovation and imagination.

> We are the South and the fire. We are inspired. We are passionate. We are heat and flame. We are the creators full of the fuel of genius and light.

> We are the West and the water. We are fluidity. We claim our tears. We are compassionate. We are the swimmers who navigate the waters of renewal and regeneration.

> We are the North and the earth. We are the soil. We are strong. We are grounded. We are the builders who manifest our dreams on the physical plane.

> We are the Above. We are the sky. We are dreamers and visionaries. We are expansive. We are magnificent. We are the gods and goddesses who create heaven here on earth.

> We are Below. We are sisters and brothers. We are the stewards. We are protectors. We are lovers. We are the healers who transmit the energy of healing through our existence.

> We are the Center. We are spirits. We are the doorway into the mysteries. We are past, present, and future. We are all that is now and was and ever will be.

> And so it is.

Teachings

This day marks the actual date when winter's temperatures begin to rise. This is a moon festival that celebrates the sexual and creative fires of the Goddess and the divine feminine. Other names for this day are Imbolg (Immolug) and Brigid's Day. Imbolc means "in the belly" and represents this time of year when the ewe's milk came in as the ewes made ready to birth their lambs. What is sacred here is the magic in the quickening of the seed that begins to grow toward the surface. This is true in nature and it is true within ourselves.

Brigid is a Celtic goddess of fire, healing, purification, and smithcraft. Her tree is the Willow, and she celebrates the art of collaboration, co-operation, and the good work of the collective. Her guides are the bees and the dove. She is all about intuition and the feminine perspective that advocates for peace.

Other goddesses that are prominent at this time of year are Vesta (Greek), who is the priestess that maintains the eternal flame. She is the goddess of our inner and outer hearth. Vesta keeps our inner fire alive. We also honor Juno (Greek). Originally this time of year marked a celebration of Juno Februata's sexual heat. The original valentines were love tickets exchanged among young people in pagan Rome, and these valentines were licentious in nature. This was considered joyous and normal. This celebration was also sacred to Hathor (Egypt), the goddess of love, passion, and sexuality.

Later the church called this Candlemas and "the feast of the Purification of the Virgin," and church fathers tried to replace the valentines with scriptural texts and even invented a St. Valentine who was a celibate bishop. This celebration was also a time for omens. Groundhog Day is based on weather predictions. In olden days, if this day was fair, more winter was to come, but if it rained, winter would not come again. Omens were taken from birds, apple peelings, tea leaves, and other sources.

Today this is a celebration in which we support each other's creative endeavors and celebrate each other. We rely on the community. Imbolg is represented by the waxing crescent moon. We release the past and grow toward our new endeavors, desires, hopes, and wishes. This is the time when we celebrate and invoke the creative spark within. We want to honor the nine muses and celebrate their creative gifts. We write poems and incantations, sing songs, dance, practice divination, and expect healing. This is a time of dedication and initiation and we expect great inner transformation. It is a time to ask for inspiration for a creative project. We recommit to our own spiritual connection to Source and we are initiated further upon the spiral path or our spiritual nature and enfoldment. We move to wake up to our fully-realized divine human potential.

Sing

Choose songs that honor the maiden aspect of the Goddess or look at appendix B for ideas.

Chant

> *What is the teaching of Imbolc? The seed is sprouting forth.*
> *Our hope comes from the light's new beginning.*
> *Behold! Our maiden Brigid is our muse.*
> *She ignites our inner flame of light.*
> *We seek the spark of her inspiration and fire.*
> *What is the teaching of Imbolc? Create.*

Read

(As each participant lights a candle at the center of the altar, read this to each of them, then have them say it out loud individually.)

> I enter here with an open
> heart and a clear mind.
> I enter new realms of creativity,
> self-expression, and brightness.
> And I give gratitude for my sisters
> and brothers and for our community.
> And so it is!

Sing

Drum and tone together to unite the energy. Choose songs that reflect our connection to the earth and invite the renewal of spring.

Read

> We call forth Brigid. She is the lady of the silver crescent
> moon. She rides her moon boat through the future waters
> of our becoming. We honor her fire and the creative spark

that she offers us for new beginnings. She is the Celtic Triple Goddess of creativity and she holds the flame of inspiration for crafting, weaving, and healing. She is our sacred and beloved muse. She fires us up to create art, poetry, music, writing, medicine, and smithcrafts. We ask Brigid to be with us tonight in ceremony.

Visit us with ideas and invention. Lead us to transformation. It is you who heal the sick with your magic and gift us with the spark of inspiration that ignites our souls. We want to infuse our lives with your passion and your bliss. Help us, oh muse, to grow into and hold your beauty and bright spirit. We want to create peace and beauty in your name. We want to heal the world. Help us to ground and protect your plan for us. Blessed be!

Silent Meditation

Turn off the lights except for the candles. Play music of your choice that is soft and dreamy. During the music ask for a short period of silence. While they sit with the music, ask your participants to ask for messages from Brigid.

Sharing

Have the participants share any relevant experiences from the silence.

Read

On this night we light the candles
Darkness gives way to the light
We call forth Brigid
She comes full of flame.
Her fire warms our hearts and hearths.
She fires our minds.
She lights up our souls.
She enlivens our spirit.

She brings forth the quickening.
She fills the air with sparks of possibility.
She sets our inspiration on fire.
Her brilliance fills us with joy.
We are filled with the passion to create.
She is our beloved muse.
The magic she offers
Is the bursting forth of the seed
Is the creating of a song
Is the writing of a poem
Is the crafting and the weaving.
She invites us to express our passion
All for the joy of the inspiration to create.
She awakens us to shine for her
To build and create in her name
To feel her ecstasy and inspiration
To dedicate our energy for peace and beauty
To be the fire
To be the passion
To be the light.
Oh Brigid, we love you and give you our gratitude.
We welcome you here.

Activity: Creating Intention

Ask your participants to close their eyes. Say: "Take a moment to feel into your heart's desires. What do you wish to create? What are you beginning? Invite the Goddess to spark the seeds of your intentions." Have each one share what that intention is.

Read

Have your group read the following either together or one by one. End with everyone saying, "And so it is."

I am a powerful and wise person.
I dedicate myself to the spirit within,
and to the power of creation and compassion.
I honor my true nature and the power
of spirit in everything that I do.
I honor my passion,
My desire to heal the earth.
I honor my own intuition and
my depths of feeling.
I honor all Mother Earth's relations.
I honor the interdependent web of all
existence of which I am a part.
I pray for peace.
I offer my creative gifts out to the
world with gratitude and thanksgiving.
Blessed be.

Divination

Pass out a bag and have each person choose an article and interpret their object, keeping in mind encouragement for the manifestation of their intention.

Sharing

Share prayers for peace and healing.

Sing

Stand and tone together. Choose a circle song that encourages creativity. Recommendations can be found in the appendix.

Read

We begin to see the effects of the returning light.
We leave the cold and dark winter.

And yet we are grateful for the quiet time
for reflection as the seed that holds the mystery
of its own growth rests deep within the earth.
And then the magic is revealed and
the seed bursts forth
We honor that mystery that allows the
spark of creation to begin anew.
We are like that seed.
We invite in new beginnings.
We embrace the muse.
We honor her by creating.
We affirm our magnificence.
We are filled with her inspiration.
We continue to build connection and community.
And to create peace and sweetness all around us.
We are open to initiations and growth.
We open our hearts and release our fears
To create endeavors and acts of healing
We dedicate ourselves again to our
individual spiritual paths.
And we honor and hold sacred the mysteries
With great joy we say, 'let the growth begin!'
And so, we release our beautiful Brigid.
We give our gratitude to her.
Blessed be.

Ending

Express your gratitude. Release the directions and open the circle.

NUIN–ASH

February 21–March 20
Fifth Lunation, February/March

Ogham: Nuin, N: ▤

Keywords: The world tree, inner and outer worlds linked, "As above, so below," macrocosm and microcosm, integrating the cosmos, the runes

Totems: Dolphins, the Hanged Man of the tarot, mermaids, water nymphs

Guides and Deities: The shaman; the priestess; Merlin; the crone aspect of the Goddess; gods and goddesses of the waters—the oceans and seas, lakes, rivers, streams, pools, ponds, and waterfalls; the Weird Sisters/the Wyrdes; Odin and the Norns (Norse); Three Fates or Moire (Greek)

Practical Guidance: Be willing to follow your inner guidance and act.

Nuin/Ash Month Ceremony

Purpose
Dive deep and retrieve your own wisdom.

Preparation

Collect a bowl of seeds of your choice. You will need a bowl filled with earth in which you can plant your seeds.

You will need a set of runes and a book to go with it. If you don't have runes you can omit this teaching aspect from the ceremony. I use the set that comes with Ralph H. Blum's book called *The Book of Runes* (St. Martin's Press, 1973) but it is a rather old source. You can also make your own set on stones or pieces of cut wood. Some books you might reference: *Nordic Runes: Understanding, Casting, and Interpreting the Ancient Viking Oracle* by Paul Rhys Mountfort and *Futhark: A Handbook of Rune Magic* by Edred Thorsson.

Welcome and Greetings

Welcome to our Ash month ceremony. Introduce yourself and go around the circle having each participant share their name and why they came to the circle. Have them close their eyes and share a moment of silence to prepare for the ceremony.

Call the Directions

Call in the directions and invoke the energies of the Ash tree (connecting the inner and outer realms) and her totems, guides, and deities (Merlin, water goddesses, the three fates, the dolphin). Set the intention of this ceremony to open the portal that will allow you to dive deep and find your own wisdom.

Teachings

The symbology of this month and the Ash tree has to do with Norse mythology. The Ash tree was named Yggdrasil, and it was known as the tree of life at the center of the world. It was during a nine-day trial that the principal Norse god Odin hung himself upside down from this tree, and through his suffering was gifted the runes from the three Norns, the goddesses of destiny. These "three maidens" resided in the Well of Urd,

The Twenty-Five Runes

1. Berkano/Growth

2. Laguz/Flow

3. Fehu/Possessions

4. Sowelo/Wholeness

5. Naudhiz/Constraint

6. Hagalaz/Disruption

7. Daguz/Breakthrough

8. Tiwaz/Warrior

9. Kaunaz/Opening

10. Perth/Initiation

11. Mannaz/The Self

12. Gebo/Partnership

13. Ingwaz/Fertility

14. Algiz/Protection

15. Raido/Journey

16. Anzus/Signals, Messages

17. Othila/Separation

18. Uraz/Strength

19. Ehwaz/Movement

20. Isa/Standstill

21. The Blank Rune, Odin's Rune/ The Unknowable

22. Thurisa/Gateway

23. Wanjo/Joy

24. Jera/Harvest

25. Eihwaz/Defense

which rested at the foot of Yggdrasil. They are known for their magical carvings or sigils on the trees, which have the ability to shape the course of destiny—one of the foremost tasks of Germanic magic. Presumably, then, Odin discovered the runes by ritually sacrificing himself and fasting for nine days while staring into the waters of the Well of Urd. It was he who imparted the runes to the first human runemasters.

The runes today are used as an oracle or divination system. The wisdom within the runes offers the spiritual warrior practices for progress and evolution. This ancient Nordic alphabet consists of twenty-four symbols and was the first system of writing developed and used by the Germanic peoples. The runes functioned as letters, but they were much more than *just* letters. Each rune is an ideographic or pictographic symbol of some cosmological principle or power, and to write a rune was to invoke and direct the force for which it stood. The runes are a vital part of the pre-Christian northern European mythology, worldview, and spiritual practice. You will find rune writing on many stones on the British Isles because of the many invasions by the Norse people. Thus, they represent another tie to the ancestors of the British Isles who used them.

Tell the story of how Odin received the runes from the three fates. You can find the story at norse-mythology.org/runes. Set the runes in a bowl and have each participant choose a rune. Read them the meaning of their rune. Remind them that this is their symbol to connect them to the inner depth and wisdom of the Ash.

Chant

> *What is the teaching of the Ash? Slow down.*
> *Our inner knowing comes from going within.*
> *Behold! We are inspired and renewed.*
> *And we are free to commune with our own divinity.*
> *We seek spiritual wisdom within the silence.*
> *What is the teaching of the Ash?*
> *Enter the doorway within your own heart.*

Guided Meditation

Now it is time for you to connect with your own inner wisdom Ash tree. Quietly go within and feed your heart flame. It is your heart center that you will connect to your inner tree. Notice your own tree. You might see, sense, or imagine your tree. This tree is your world tree and you have the keys you need to enter it. Within this tree is all the guidance and knowledge you will ever need. There is nothing outside of yourself that is more magnificent or amazing.

Stand in front of your tree and look up to see how tall it is. See its root system that you stand upon stretch out in all directions. See a golden door that is built into the tree and is big enough for you to enter. Notice that you hold a set of golden keys in your hand. Find the key that attracts your attention and know that it is the key that will open the tree's door. Go ahead and use the key to open the door. As you stand at the threshold see bright white light that is most welcoming. Take a moment to adjust to the light before you enter. Take off your shoes and leave them at the entrance.

As you walk into the tree begin to feel the beauty and presence of this tree. Find that you are both the microcosm and the macrocosm. You are all and everything and you are in oneness. Here you receive the understanding that you have never been separate. Take a moment to simply open to this communication.

Sit down and breathe deeply. As you sit here quietly in the heart of your tree, begin to connect with your own heart. As you honor your central flame you feed it with love. As you do this your heart flame grows and fills you with warmth and appreciation. Listen very carefully for that small central voice at the core of yourself that lives here. Listen to its messages and to its concerns. Simply lend your ear ... (pause)

Be willing to quiet your mind, which is so concerned with its judgments, comparisons, and analysis. Be willing to rest in surrender to beauty, peace, harmony, and love. You may remember music, songs, books, or poems that have moved you. You may remember what has inspired you. Think for a moment about what really feeds you and what you most enjoy. Here at the center you find inspiration, the courage to be yourself, and the ability to connect with your own heart. Take a moment to really remember who you are and what you truly love … (long pause)

As this journey completes itself give your gratitude to your inner tree. Honor your world tree and let it know that you intend to spend time with it. Know that you can create the next chapter of your life in a good way. Are you ready to act upon your inner guidance and walk your talk? Are you prepared to stay close to your heart and feel the power of possibility and intention toward your good? Are you prepared to share this good in the future as this is the fruit that will grow from your own tree?

Sharing

Come back into this time and into this place from which you originally journeyed and write your experiences in your journal. Make sure you ground and center. Have the participants share their experiences with the group.

Activity: Retrieving Information and Planting Our Desires for Manifestation

Take a moment and have each person remember something they learned or received from their own inner counsel, their own inner tree. What did each person receive? This could be a word, a smile, a vision, a feeling, a blessing, quietude …

Say: "And so, when we have retrieved authentic information from our depths, what can we do with it? What will we manifest or create? Think of one thing you can do with your gift. Think of one change, one decision, one thought, feeling, or action that you could make to help bring this gift out into the world to share."

Pass out a bowl of seeds and ask each person to take one. Go around the circle and have the participants share what they desire to manifest. Then have them plant that seed in a communal earthen bowl, filled with rich dirt, that sits at the central altar in the middle of the circle. After each person plants their seed have the group respond together with "And so it is!"

Read

Now that you have planted your seed, your tree of manifestation will bud, and blossom come spring, and by summer your tree will grow fruit, and the fruit will be the keys of light that you share because they were fostered from within your true essence.

Ending

Release the directions and open the circle with gratitude for the Ash tree and its helpers.

An Ash Story: My Totem Dolphin Saved My Life

This is a story that demonstrates the power of working with the totems of the trees. I was driving home from work one day and thinking I would like to get down to writing about my experiences with the dolphin as a totem animal, and in the next instant, a truck pulled up alongside of me and on its side was a large picture of a beautiful dolphin with the word *dolphin* spelled out. I like to take these synchronicities as signs of encouragement.

And so, I begin! I have always enjoyed stories and pictures and movies about dolphins, but I have never felt a close identification with them on a conscious level. I have never been swimming with the dolphins or even seen them from a boat, like so many people have. And yet my inner dolphin has certainly sustained me and shared with me. My first encounter with my totem dolphin saved my life!

At the age of forty, I was working part-time teaching troubled high school dropouts, attending graduate school in psychology, parenting my challenging six-year-old son, getting a divorce, living on a shoestring financially, and partying whenever I could fit it in and when my son was with his father. My last class course before my counseling internship was on drug and alcohol addiction and that's when I began to understand that I had a problem with alcohol. My relationship with my boyfriend had just ended with his decision to leave for India, and I was feeling alone, raw, and vulnerable. I was falling through the cracks of my life.

After a series of embarrassing fiasco party events, which occurred under the influence of alcohol, and feeling engulfed by the incredible pain of where my life was in the moment, I had reached the bottom. The pain and grief I was experiencing seemed too great to endure any longer. It was as if the weight of all the emotional debris of my life was hitting me with a tidal wave force, and I had no legs to stand on, let alone anything to hold on to. I seriously considered death as a viable option.

I remember the night when I realized I could not go on. I made a prayer to the universe asking for help. I felt that without some sense of guidance or support I would not go on with my life. It was with great clarity that I made my prayer. I admitted to myself that I was abusing alcohol and that I drank to kill the pain of my life. I felt such shame and failure. With this on my mind, I fell into a deep sleep. I have never experienced such a deep sense of futility and self-loathing.

Upon awakening, I recalled the most intensely real and actualizing dream. That night, my "porpoise" came to me. I stood on the edge of a vast ocean. Rather close to shore, a bottle popped up in the waves. It was a vodka bottle, and in it was my mother.

My mom was an active alcoholic in the last years of her life, and she died of accidental drowning probably due to a blackout experienced while she was swimming alone in shallow water. Her favorite drink was vodka.

From the bottle, my mother beckoned me. She called my name in a sweet seductive voice that flowed like honey. Her hand extended from the bottle and she signaled for me to come to her.

It was crystal clear in the dream that if I followed her, I too would drown. The bottle was a trap, and not a vehicle for managing or navigating the ocean of emotion and the unconscious. As much as I desired to join my mother and follow the seductive call, I clearly and adamantly decided not to go toward her. In that moment of decision my dream changed, and I found myself sailing in a boat, moving along on aquamarine water at a fast speed. I noticed the sail catching the wind and the vast blue sky and the bright, full sun above. The air was full of the smell of the sea salt and the crisp cut of the wind. Above me was a beautiful kite, sailing high along with the movement of the boat and the wind.

In the myth of Osiris, Isis comes to her dead husband's body as an Egyptian bird—a kite. She flies to him and, through her magic, becomes impregnated by him to give birth to their spiritual son, Horus. I had originally thought that she had come as a kite, the toy that we play with as children, because I didn't know anything about Egyptian birds. And that is the way that I had always imagined the story. To me the kite in my dream was Isis, the mother of the world, who brings the power of new life and the infusion of spiritual meaning and healing. She portends resurrection.

Next to come in the dream was a beautiful porpoise or dolphin. She showed up as my purpose! She swam alongside for a while and then she came up to the back of the boat. The boat slowed down enough for her to rise out of the water and hover above it so that she could meet me at eye level. Her eyes were filled with a powerful unconditional love that filled my being and soul. She was full of merriment and unconditional acceptance and care. She restored me. My pain broke into a million pieces and dissolved. In exchange she offered me faith and hope.

There I was, clearly navigating the waters of my life. The air and the wind were my intellect, my inspiration and aspiration, and my ability to communicate. The kite was my connection to the divine feminine and my Egyptian spiritual lineage. The boat was my vessel, my own life, riding on top of the water. The porpoise was a guide and supreme transmitter of consciousness, who modeled for me how I could navigate my life. I did not need to live in my pain and sorrow. The porpoise was my companion and totem. Her spiritual sensitivity and dedication to service was my clue. I was to navigate the water of emotion in a different way than my mother had chosen, and I had lots of help!

After going through the memory of this powerful dream that morning, I knew that my prayer had been heard and responded to. I was filled with new purpose, hope, and understanding. I was not alone! I felt rejuvenated and I clearly understood that alcohol was a trap and would lead me to a wasted life. And so, dolphin became my personal guide, and this was long before I knew anything about totems. Dolphin saved my life, strengthened me, filled me with love, and put me back on a path to health and thriving.

You too can connect with your totems. Think about the synchronicities in your life. What are the messages? What is the encouragement? If you have a deep need of healing because of a wound that is interfering in your life—and we all do—sit in meditation before you go to sleep. Ask your most authentic self for the guidance you are seeking. Ask for the transmission of healing and love. You may not receive a dream right away, but you will begin to see signs and signals like the dolphin showing up on the side of a truck when I considered writing about my healing experience with the dolphin. Interesting that the dolphin as the totem of the Ash is representative of diving deep into the waters of the self and uniting with the larger definition of *self*, our identity as spirit.

Ash navigates the waters between the worlds. When we pick up the phone line, whether through dreams, visions, meditations, knowing or sensing, or synchronicities, we hook up to our wiser, unconditionally loving self. That is who we really are. Meditate on the world tree, the Ash, and all her helpers. See yourself as the tree. Know that you are connected to below and above and with the inner and the outer. You are built to receive this regeneration and renewal if you but ask and open yourself to it. Be open to finding out about your own helpers. Look to the creatures that show up in the world around you and in your dream life. What totems are you already attracted to? They are probably already on your team just waiting for an invitation to become better friends and allies to you.

HUATHE–HAWTHORN

March 21–April 17
Sixth Lunation, April

Ogham: Huathe (hoh'uh), H: ⊣

Keywords: Cleansing, purity, chastity, protection of the inner realm, preparation for Beltane, the sacred marriage between intellect/mind and feeling/intuition, spring cleaning, the fairy tree

Totems: Fairies, the White Stag, unicorn

Guides and Deities: Herne the Hunter, Cernunnos the Horned God, the Green Man of the woods, maiden goddesses—Kernal, the Great Queen, Mother Goddesses—Ker

Practical Guidance: Clean up your act. Apply discipline and restraint.

Huathe/Hawthorn Month Ceremony
Holiday
The Spring Equinox/Ostara is March 20/21.

Purpose

To celebrate the Hawthorn portal and the return of spring. The intention of this ceremony is to commune with the unseen world and to enter the realm of magic. This is also an opportunity to return to your innocence and reestablish your own sacred sovereignty. You can use this ceremony to encourage cleansing and clearing.

Welcome and Greetings

Welcome to our Hawthorn month ceremony. Introduce yourself and go around the circle having each participant share their name and why they came to the circle. Have them close their eyes and share a moment of silence to prepare for the ceremony.

Call the Directions

Call in the directions and invoke the energies of the Hawthorn tree (cleansing and purification) and her totems, guides, and deities (the White Stag, the elfin people, the fairies/faeries, the unicorn, the Priestess of the Hawthorn tree, Herne the Hunter, Cernunnos, the Green Man, the maiden and mother goddesses). We give our gratitude to the elementals that help sustain life upon the planet. Invoke the spirit of the Hawthorn trees. Give gratitude to all the helpers in the unseen realm for their work in creating and maintaining the physical manifestation of the flora on the planet. We are also able to celebrate the balance of this time of year between the solar and the lunar influences. We celebrate Kernal's return from the underworld and Ker's joy at her daughter's return. We honor the springtime.

Teachings

The Hawthorn is known as the fairy tree. She is protective of what we hold sacred. She reminds us to hold our inner life as sacred and to view our bodies as sacred. She also provides protection for the magical realm from the harsh judgments and ridicule that come from a mental linear approach to life that has no room for the mystical. She reminds us to return to our innocence and open to the mysteries. She reminds us that Mother Earth is a paradise and we are here to honor her. We are grateful for the return of the sun and the blooming beginnings of the new life cycle. This is a purification month during which cleansing was a vital way of preparing for Beltane on May 1, which was the beginning of summer and the planting season for the Celts. This is where our spring cleaning idea comes from.

Chant

> What is the teaching of the Hawthorn? Magic is afoot.
> Our joy comes from our relationship with the natural world.
> Behold! We purify and prepare. We cleanse as spring returns.
> And we are free to dance within the mystery.
> We seek understanding of our sacred sovereignty.
> What is the teaching of the Hawthorn? Return to innocence.

Sing

Choose songs that honor the Goddess in her many forms as well as songs to initiate the turning of the wheel and the return of the sun and springtime.

Guided Meditation

To begin to reestablish your connection to your own innocence and sovereignty, close your eyes. Imagine yourself as someone who is worthy of protection and respect... Take a moment to let that sink in. Breathe these words into yourself. Are you willing to make a commitment to yourself to be your own advocate? If you are so willing, make that silent commitment to yourself right now ... (pause)

Go back to a scene in which you were wronged or misjudged as a child. Take a moment to really be in that moment from the past... (pause) Now see your adult self enter this memory as your special advocate. Allow your adult self to stand up for your younger self and say things that you were unable or too small to say. Give this process a few moments … (pause)

From now on, let it be known that for anything that occurred in the past, or will occur in the future, your adult self will be present to defend, protect, and comfort your child self. And let it be known that this kind of visualization is so powerful that it changes the past and puts your present and future on a different track and a stronger foundation. Any memory of harm to your self-esteem or sense of safety can be transformed. This is your key to regaining your own sense of self-empowerment no matter what wounding has occurred in the past. Send love to your child self and to your adult self and let that sink in.

Now take this opportunity to identify any emotional baggage that you are ready to let go of.

Take the time that you need … (pause)

Now in your mind's eye you begin to see or imagine yourself in a beautiful glade of trees and flowers. There are forest animals and all kinds of magical creatures around you. This is a place of great safety and joy. With your inner sight imagine a field that hosts a lovely grove of Hawthorn trees. It is early spring and the sun is shining. It feels good to be out of doors again and to feel the warmth of the sun.

The trees are filled with their red, pink, or white flowers and you notice a special aura around the grove. You can view this as you see the trees from afar. You remember that the Hawthorn is magical, and is known as the fairy tree. As you walk closer to the grove you seem to lose track of space and time. You begin to experience a giddy feeling of joy and bliss. You enter the grove and hear the many tiny little beings that are dancing and frolicking. They do not seem surprised by your presence and they beckon you to join them. You hesitate for a moment and decide to sit down and enjoy the festivities from the side, as you need time to adjust to your new environment and the magic of this place.

You notice that you are carrying a large sack that holds that which you may be ready to let go of. This bag is full of heavy memories and situations that have harmed or grieved or enraged or disappointed you.

In this bag are all the feelings that engender a sense of hopelessness and pain.

Lovely little fairies come to gather the bag that holds these dense energy patterns. They smile at you and ask if you are ready to release this burden. If you say yes, they will take your bag from your shoulders and then simply return to the void to empty the contents back into the realm of all possibilities. If you are not prepared to let go, this is fine as well. But this is a good day to let go...

See and feel yourself free of this emotional weight, or at least much lighter. You see yourself free and joyful. Fully feel the joy of not having that weight upon your shoulders. Perhaps you see yourself dancing a little jig of joy! Give gratitude to your helpful little fairies!

The fairies want to remind you to believe in magic just like you used to when you were a very small child. They tell you to look for their signs in mushroom circles and fast flitting movements when you think you see them, but then they are gone. They let you know that the hummingbirds, dragonflies, butterflies, and even the frogs are a reminder that magic exists. Their sounds help to break up dense energy. Take a moment to listen to further messages that they might have for you...(pause)

Their last message to you is to remember them. They ask you to support wild places where they are free and not bothered by humans. They ask for your gratitude as well. After all, it is a lot to do all that they do without recognition. They suggest that perhaps there is a little corner of your own yard or garden that you can leave wild for them.

It is now time that you must leave this special place. Again, give your gratitude and love to every creature. Give your gratitude to the Hawthorns. Know that you can return to this magical place anytime you want. As you say your goodbyes, begin to return your attention to your own time and your own place. Bring your attention back into your body and ground and center.

Sharing

It is now time to ground and center and to return to this time and this space. Record your experiences in your journal. Pass the talking stick and share your experiences.

Activity: Choosing a Symbolic Act of Release

Say: "It is also time to think about a symbolic act that demonstrates that you have released burdens that you no longer wish to carry. Choose something that you are prepared to do when you get home. This may be cleaning your closet or drawers or letting go of something that carries memories that are disheartening. You might have a garage sale, give things away to friends, or take a load to Goodwill. In this way, you set your own intention and agree to participate in an actual current mundane physical cleansing of some sort. This grounds the experience into your everyday life reality."

Give them some time to close their eyes and think about this. Pass the talking stick so they can state their intention.

Have your participants close their eyes for just a moment. Have them imagine a grove of Hawthorn trees. Have them notice that the trees begin to sway and that the leaves rustle loudly in the wind.

The trees begin to whisper a message: "Consider our thorns for a moment. Our thorns are a powerful symbol to help you remember to protect that which is most sacred to you. We the Hawthorn trees want you to know that we will protect you from harm and keep safe that which is vulnerable to you. We offer you our love and our magic and our support. Are you willing to honor your belief in the unseen world? Give your gratitude for the important work that is done by the creatures in the creation and maintenance of life on the planet. The creatures of this realm want us to remind you that it does no good to argue with those humans who are not able to believe in this unseen dimension. But those who do are blessed!"

Sing

Choose a closing song such as "May the Circle Be Open," "Merry Meet," or "We Are a Circle," or songs that honor nature and springtime.

Ending

Release the directions and give your gratitude to the totems, guides, and deities and to the Hawthorn. Open the circle with gratitude.

A Hawthorn Story: The Unicorn as an Ally

This is a story of how the unicorn totem helped a dear family member when she was recovering from surgery. She had a cancerous tumor removed from her third eye area, was scheduled for radiation treatment, and was not looking forward to this regimen.

I agreed to lead her in guided visualizations to see if we could connect with some helpers from the magical realms. Indeed, a unicorn appeared in my sister-in-law's journey. In her mind's eye, a graceful white unicorn appeared in a green field. He was stately and regal, and she could describe him to me. He looked at her with intense love and understanding. He communicated with her telepathically. He told her that he would be with her through her treatments and that she could keep her focus upon him. He would provide courage and a connection to the world of magic, joy, and healing.

Her radiation treatment involved an intense schedule that consisted of daily treatments over the course of many, many weeks. She was placed in a mask that held her head tightly in place so that she couldn't move. This allowed the area of her forehead to be exactly targeted. At first the mask was intolerable and suffocating and she suffered acute claustrophobia. She also was told not to move, and she has always had a persistent cough. She wondered how in the world she was going to manage not coughing.

From her very first treatment, her unicorn appeared in her mind's eye and began to communicate with her. He asked her to focus her attention on him. While doing this she began to relax, and she was able to move into a dream state. During the treatment she found that she could drift out of her body and into a blissful experience. In this relaxed state she had no need to cough.

Throughout her treatments, the appearance of her ally the unicorn was a signal to relax and calm herself. The unicorn also provided her with a connection to courage that she needed in order to keep showing up for more treatments. He engaged her in an experience of magic, peacefulness, and childlike wonder. The feeling that he brought to her through each treatment carried her through.

It is synchronistic to me that the unicorn appeared for her with his amazing spiraled horn coming from his forehead. Was this the perfect ally for healing the exact area in which my sister-in-law was having trouble? Did he stimulate her third eye as a means of involving her in her own healing process? Upon the end of her treatments, the MRI showed no more cancer there. She was extremely grateful to the unicorn and he is a staunch protector and ally for her to this day!

I offered this assistance over the phone, as my sister-in-law lived far away. We both just closed our eyes and I asked her to find a lovely spot in nature in her mind's eye. Then I asked her what she was seeing, suggesting that a helper would show up for her. Indeed, a unicorn appeared. I asked her to describe it in detail and tell me what it was doing. She had no problem with this. Then I prompted her to ask her unicorn if he would help her through her medical procedures. He said yes. She asked for more information, which he gave her. She was to concentrate on him during her medical sessions and he would transport her on a lovely journey. And this was a huge relief to her. We thanked him and then both opened our eyes and returned to our phone conversation.

It is my belief, born out of this experience, that usual medical procedures can be combined with energetic healing practices to help the patient get through these intense and difficult treatment protocols and to enhance the recovery process. And how wonderful to connect with the magical realm and have the help of this most beautiful ally.

You can do this for yourself or you can lead someone through a guided meditation. The inner life has such wisdom. The exact correct totem or guide will appear. You just need to set your intention and make some quiet space to journey, then be willing to receive the information.

If you yourself are going through a difficult time, or if you know someone who is, you might offer a guided meditation to find a helper for the situation. The helper that shows up can offer guidance for how best to move through the challenge.

It is quite possible to connect with the unseen helpers of the elemental world. If you but ask they will show up and gift you with real tangible support and healing. Another way to strengthen your relationships with the magical realm is to read stories and poems and fairy tales that depict the little people and magical creatures. Sit beneath a Hawthorn tree. Gather flowers and bring them inside. Gather pictures around you of the flower fairies. The elementals will be grateful and flow their delightful sense of mirth your way.

Fairy tales are full of totem helpers and life teaching themes. One way to meet up with your own magic helpers or to get in touch with your own central life theme is to write your own fairy tale. By doing so you put yourself directly in the hands of magic. If you simply allow the writing to occur without censorship, there is a magical story waiting for you. It will write itself because it comes from within. It has a message for you, and for others. You will be amazed. Pick up a pen and set your intention to write your own tale. You might start with the words "Once upon a time," then pick a place, pick a character, and let the magic flow. Have fun with it.

Hawthorn invites you to open to the magic. Our imaginations are linked to her. Hawthorn is a fairy tree and all the creatures of our fables and fairy tales live under her. She protects them. She reminds us that we are part of the magic unfolding. She is a doorway into our own ability to play and frolic and enjoy ourselves. Stories are a part of this. Sit under a Hawthorn and see what comes to you as you daydream away. As you imagine your own story, what are the themes that come forth from your own imagination? What blueprints are offered up for your life?

Spring Equinox Ceremony
March 20/21

The Spring Equinox is a day of equal day and equal night; it marks the end of the dark half of the year and the beginning of the waxing cycle. We honor the maiden aspect of the Goddess and the rebirth of the earth. It is a day of perfect balance.

Purpose

To celebrate the Spring Equinox. To experience a position of neutrality or balance.

Preparation

Have your participants bring their journals or pass them pencils, pens, and paper. Prepare a bowl of seeds of your choice and provide a large bowl of earth in which the seeds can be planted.

Welcome and Greetings

Welcome to our Spring Equinox ceremony. Introduce yourself and go around the circle having each participant share their name and why they came to the circle. Have them close their eyes and share a moment of silence to prepare for the ceremony.

Call the Directions

Call in the energy of this day. Call in the maiden aspect of the Goddess and give gratitude for the return of the sun and the beginning of the spring.

Teachings

We call this holiday the vernal equinox, Alban Eiler, Easter, or Ostara. We now begin the season of preparation and the planting of the seeds. The name *Easter* comes from the Saxon fertility goddess Ostara. The hare and eggs are symbols of the regenerative power that is offered at this time. We celebrate the fertility of nature.

We now officially begin a time of cleansing and purification or making ready for Beltane on May 1. Spring cleaning on a physical, emotional, mental, and spiritual level is in order. It is time to clean your house. We celebrate the warming of the earth and the seeds that grow to sprouting and budding after the long hibernation. This is a time when we consider the following:

- Initiations
- Making wishes for the renewal of hope
- Creativity
- Wisdom
- Success in a project
- Better relationships
- Wishes and dreams for ourselves, for others, and for the world
- Vows
- Expectations and new possibilities

Sing

Choose songs of hope and light that celebrate the Goddess.

Chant

What is the teaching of the Spring Equinox? Celebrate.
Our renewal comes from the return of the maiden to her mother.
Behold! We celebrate new life and the growing green world.
We are free to enjoy the blessings of the sun's return.
We seek to share our gratitude.
What is the teaching of the Spring Equinox? Be joyful.

Sharing

This is a time to appreciate our own successes and fertility. It is a time for giving gratitude. Have your group think about something they've recently accomplished and are proud of, something that they've gotten through that was challenging, or something that each is grateful for. They can write these things down in their journals. Pass the talking stick and have them share.

Guided Meditation

This is a time when there is a balance between the dark and the light half of the year. It suggests that there is a middle road, a more neutral, less subjective, more objective position that one can take when dealing with polarity. A wonderful example of this is "the Seat of Neutrality," which is an actual place in the Temple of Kom Ombo in Egypt. This temple was built to honor both Sobek (the Egyptian crocodile god of chaos), who represents the dark, and Horus (the Egyptian falcon god of empowerment), who represents the light—holding the tension of the light and the dark in wholeness without judgment. Built right down the center of the temple is a seat that allows the initiate to sit in the middle of all opposition and polarity. It is wonderful to sit on this stone seat and experience this place of balance and perfect neutrality.

Imagine yourself traveling to this beautiful temple in Egypt and walking into the interior of the temple. Here you will see the Seat of Neutrality that is settled smack between two gods and two temples. Go ahead and step up to the stone seat that sits like a niche carved into a rock wall standing between the two temples. Hoist yourself up to the stone seat and take some time to meditate here. Simply be in this space without any attachment to the two sides of light and dark, good and bad, and any polarity you might be experiencing in your life. Simply be in the in between place that is dedicated to this middle way. (Allow them time to have their experience.)

It is now time to return from this optimum place of inner balance and perception. Give your gratitude knowing that you can return to this place and this experience anytime you so desire. It exists strongly in etheric form and is here to help you navigate polarity and help you practice acceptance of what is. This is a good state of mind to remember when life becomes very unbalanced and the negative seems to outweigh the positive.

Sharing

When they return from this guided journey have them share their experiences with the Seat of Neutrality.

Activity: Planting Seeds for the Future of the Community

Pass around a bowl of seeds. Each person takes a seed and meditates on what they want to plant for the future. This is your community bowl that fosters cooperation and mutuality and these are seeds for the future. After a time of silence ask each of them to share as they plant their seed in a large bowl, filled with earth, that's sitting in the center. After each person speaks and shares what they are planting, the group responds with "And so it is!"

Sing

Choose a song that reflects balance, healing, or the mystery.

Ending

Have each person place their prayers for healing into the center. Open the circle and release the directions.

DUiR~OAK

April 18–May 15
Seventh Lunation, May

Ogham: Duir (der or dur), D: ᚇ

Keywords: Strength, stability, protection and grounding, doorway to the mysteries, fertility, sexuality, spring, thresholds, eggs, flowers, initiations and initiates

Totems: The White Stag, bull, rabbit or hare

Guides and Deities: Gaia—Mother Earth, the maiden aspect of the Goddess, Herne the Hunter, Cernunnos, and the Great Goddess

Practical Guidance: Do not underestimate your own strength. The key to opening your own spiritual door is your strength.

Duir/Oak Month Ceremony

Holiday
Beltane is May 1.

Purpose

To celebrate the portal of the Oak month.

Preparation

Procure a bowl of acorns. Prepare a bowl of earth large enough to hold candles for your group. Gather a larger central candle and enough smaller candles for your group.

Welcome and Greetings

Welcome to our Oak month ceremony. Introduce yourself and go around the circle having each participant share their name and why they came to the circle. Have them close their eyes and share a moment of silence to prepare for the ceremony.

Call in the Directions

Call in the directions and invoke the energies of the Oak tree (strength, spring, sacred union) and her totems, guides, and deities (the bull, the White Stag, Herne the Hunter, Cernunnos, the Great Goddess).

Teachings

The Oak portal celebrates fertility. Doorways and thresholds hold special significance. All around us the flowers and trees are blooming. The renewal has begun. Beauty is everywhere. We honor the fairies and the elfin people and the unseen realm. We give our gratitude to the devas and dryads of each plant and tree species who organize and protect every aspect of the seasonal growth. This is a time for magic and gaiety, frolic and merriment. This tree offers us grounding, strength, and stability.

Read

We honor the maiden as well as new growing generations. We honor Gaia our Mother Earth. We celebrate the renewal of her life force. All around us is new growth in the buds and blossoms of springtime.

Chant

What is the teaching of the Oak? Fertility.
Our renewal comes from the maiden's return from the underworld.
Behold! We honor the fairies and the elfin people.
And we are free to create life itself and to make merry.
We seek to celebrate together in joy.
What is the teaching of the Oak? Create and enjoy.

Sing

Choose songs that celebrate spring.

Activity: The Acorn and New Beginnings

Before the journey begins, pass around a bowl of acorns. Have each person take an acorn. Then say: "Let this acorn represent what it is you want to begin and grow now in your life. What would you like to grow from this little acorn?" (Long pause)

Ask them to close their eyes for a moment and say: "Your dreams and desires and goals are no less than an actual child of your flesh, for they are part of you and seek expression in the world. As you grow your goals and desires, how will you honor them?" (Pause)

Guided Meditation

As you hold your acorn in your hand, close your eyes and we'll begin to take a beautiful journey together. Slow your breathing down and center yourself at your heart. Feed your heart with love. Let go of your worries and concerns. Take another deep breath. Feel your acorn.

You find yourself in a lovely green field full of trees and flowers. The sun is bright and you hear the birds as they swoop and fly above; you see the fluffy white clouds move gently through the blue sky. This is a magical place and you feel very safe. The colors are vibrant and alive, and you feel at home here.

You walk through the field until you come to a special spot. It is here that you can plant the acorn of your dreams and desires. Take the time that you need to dig a hole for your acorn. When you are ready, you can place your acorn in the hole, add some magical fertilizer, and place the dirt over it. Make your special prayers. Perhaps you find a watering can right there and you can sprinkle the area in which you have planted your special acorn. Hold your hands over the spot and give your acorn some love and positive energy.

Imagine now that your tree begins to grow, and you observe it growing and growing until it becomes a mighty oak. We fast-forward into the future. Watch it as its trunk thickens and grows forth branches that begin to fill the area above the tree with leaves. Watch as the leaves and limbs reach farther and farther toward the sky and take up more and more space. See the root system grow down deeper into the earth. Feel the magnitude of this huge Oak that has grown to its full stature right before your eyes. Take a moment to realize that you are the steward of this tree. Feed your tree with love and appreciation.

Notice that a group of friends has come to help you celebrate the growth of your tree. Totems, guides, and deities from the spirit world may also show up. The fairies present themselves. All join hands with you and you all begin to sing and dance around your Oak tree. When the joyful dance is done they continue to hold a circle for you as they witness you moving close to your tree. They invite you to take a moment to embrace your tree and touch it. The tree emanates its communication and you receive the communication...

Now imagine that the acorn you have planted also has grown your own dreams and desires. Fast-forward the manifestation of a special dream just like you fast-forwarded the growth of the Oak tree. Take a moment to take in the future vision to see the fruit of your own dream come true ... (pause) Now go ahead and feel the joy of having manifested your heart's desire. Celebrate the manifestation in your mind's eye.

When you feel complete give your gratitude to all your friends and helpers. Give your gratitude to your Oak, and for your own dreams and desires. Begin to return and ground and center. When you are ready and back to the present time and place, gently open your eyes.

Sharing

Give them time to record their journey in their journals and then allow each participant to share. What message did they receive from their tree? What was it like to see the acorn grow to its full potential? What goal or heart desire did they see manifested in their journey? What did it feel like to see that dream come true?

Sing

Choose some songs that have to do with spring, fertility, the Goddess, abundance, joy, and celebration.

Activity: Sharing Our Goals and Aspirations

Have each participant light a candle at the center that represents a goal or aspiration that they choose to focus on to bring into manifestation. After each one lights their candle and shares, all the participants respond with: "We witness you. We support you. We love you."

Sing

Stand, join hands, and sing some ending circle songs such as "May the Circle Be Open," "Merry Meet," and "We Are a Circle," or choose songs that honor the spring and the maiden aspect of the Goddess.

Endings

Release the directions and give your gratitude to the Oak and to her totems, guides, and deities. Have your participants take their acorn home. They can plant it or place it upon their altar to remind them of their goals and aspirations. Open the circle.

An Oak Story: My Birth Tree

The month of May is my favorite time of year and I am a May baby. I love the profusion of flowers budding and the activity of the birds singing me awake every morning. May carries a promise of fertility and everywhere there is evidence of growing life. The animals have their babies and the fields and trees blossom. The sun is out and the air is warm. What a relief. We have made it through another winter.

My favorite tree is the Oak. It is my birth tree. It is so sturdy and can grow to such a huge stature. I love the little acorn and am always reminded of what can grow from just a seed. This is the time of year that I think about what I am growing. How am I doing? Is there more that I need to take care of to ensure that my goals and aspirations will be met? I love to meet with my women friends in circle, as we always talk about our projects and seek support. It is indeed their support that so feeds me. We meet at least once a month. If you don't have such a group, I suggest that you form one. I simply asked like-minded friends to join me and eventually each person took responsibility for running a circle. Just like the ceremonies that I have included in this book, the women brought their own ideas and we all enjoyed it. One of the things that we often lack in our busy world is a safe place in which we can be authentic. Such a circle is an answer to this.

I once had a special dream about an Oak. The dream took place in the forest, and I found myself in a cozy little home inside of a huge Oak tree. The entrance to my home had a little door with a curved top and toward the top there was a little round window in it. Outside I heard a commotion and the sounds of angry words. I looked through the window and I saw young men who were angry and yelling at me to come out and fight. They beat at my door and pounded with their fists and kicked their feet against it. At first I was frightened by their aggression and hostility, so I chose to stay inside the tree, but I could see them through the little round window in the door. They kept hollering and began to bang even more loudly and threateningly at my door. I felt frightened and very small.

Finally, I was angry because they kept bothering me and they wouldn't go away, so I went out the door (the duir) and was calm and collected. One by one, I kicked their butts, with hardly any effort at all. I met their force and used martial arts; I flipped them over and derailed each angry, hostile young man. Rather than meeting their force directly, I used the force of their own aggression as it moved them past me. They went home exhausted and defeated, "never to darken my door again!"

When I awakened from this dream I felt energized and charged with positive force. I discovered that taking action in a dream could effect change in my daily waking life. The dream gifted me with an infusion of positive energy and self-empowerment!

I found that I was less fearful of aggression and that I had a way to navigate through an experience with someone who may be very aggressive or threatening. It is not that I know exactly what to do, so much as knowing that I should trust my instincts and not use aggressive force. I already have a blueprint for how to get through the situation and triumph.

After the dream, there was a situation that showed up in my waking life in which I was able to apply the healing instructions of my dream. I had gone to a new service station that told me I needed a new water pump, which they then replaced. It so happened that in getting an oil change at my usual old car repair place they found out I did not actually need a new water pump.

Empowered with the energy of the dream, I was able to go back to the service station, present the facts, reverse the charges, and replace my original water pump, which I had kept. Usually I would cringe at the idea of going back to an all-male blue-collar workplace and having to stand up for myself. Yet I was able to get my money back, have my original water pump put back, and get their apologies. And I did this without fear and without resorting to aggression or threats.

Dreams are potentially powerful healing tools. Do not dismiss their messages, nor their healing ability. They are direct communications with our inner wisdom and guidance through metaphor. Symbols have a way of cutting through the intellect. Ask for a powerful dream and you will get one. Ask the trees for messages and they will show up in your dreams.

I also suggest that you begin to develop a special relationship with your birth tree. You can find your own birth tree from the chart below. Once you have identified your tree or trees (as two months share a tree) you can become more familiar with its attributes and teachings and can develop a closer friendship with it.

If your birthday falls between:	Your birth tree is:
November 1–November 28	Birch
November 29–December 26	Rowan
December 27–January 23	Alder
January 24–February 20	Willow
February 21–March 20	Ash
March 21–April 17	Hawthorn
April 18–May 15	Oak
May 16–June 12	Holly
June 13–July 10	Hazel & Apple*
July 11–August 7	Vine
August 8–September 4	Ivy
September 5–October 2	Reed & Blackthorn**
October 3–October 30	Elder
October 31	The Grove***

* The Quert Apple shares the month with the Coll Hazel, so those who have these birthdays can claim both trees.

** The Straif Blackthorn shares the month with Reed, so those who have these birthdays can claim both trees.

*** Those who were born on October 31 can claim the Grove, which stands for a group of trees and can represent any kind of tree you choose. This date relates to a very important day in Celtic cosmology, one on which we can claim our connection to spirit.

Beltane Ceremony
May 1

Beltane is the Celtic fire cross-quarter holiday to initiate the growing season and begin the Celtic light half of the year. We celebrate fertility. This date in the Celtic past signifies the beginning of summer and the time for sowing seeds. The purpose of the ritual was to ensure a healthy crop and a bountiful harvest in the late summer and fall.

Purpose

To celebrate Beltane.

Welcome and Greetings

Welcome to our Beltane ceremony. Introduce yourself and go around the circle having each participant share their name and why they came to the circle. Have them close their eyes and share a moment of silence to prepare for the ceremony.

Call the Directions

Call in the energies of Beltane. We honor fertility and the renewal of life. Call in the fairies and give them gratitude for the help they provide for the growth of the flora upon our earth. Call in the maiden aspect of the Goddess.

Teachings

Today we too are grateful for the return of the sun and the abundance that we are offered.

We honor the fairies and the elfin people and the unseen realm. We give our gratitude to the devas and dryads of each plant and tree species who organize and protect every aspect of the seasonal growth. This is a time for magic and gaiety, frolic and merriment. This is the night that we honor the maiden as well as new growing generations. We honor Gaia, our Mother Earth. We honor sexuality, sensuality, progeny, and the miracle of birth. We celebrate the renewal of her life force. All around us is new growth in the buds and blossoms of springtime.

Beltane marks the change that moves a maiden forward into the fires of her own sexuality. Spring flowers are used to commemorate the classical drama of the maiden's blossom-time and return from the underworld. The names of some of the universal maiden Goddesses of this return are Kore, Flora, Freya (Scandinavian), Blodeuwedd, and Persephone (Greek). Flowers are the symbol of the season as well as symbols for female sexuality.

The Maypole dance is a part of this celebration. The Maypole represents a gigantic phallus planted in Mother Earth to fructify her womb. The ribbons of different colors are used to braid over and under around the pole as participants passing on the inside must duck under the ribbons carried by those who are moving on the outside of the circle, and then shift places as they continue moving in opposite directions around the Maypole. The weaving represents the weft and warp of our lives and loves.

We celebrate the weaving of the universe into existence by Spider Woman (Native American). We honor the blooming and passion of both the coming-of-age goddess and the earth herself. This is also a time for celebrating sisterhood. And we celebrate romantic love and attraction, which ensures sexuality leading to the mystery of fertility and progeny. The custom of making love in the fields on May Eve was done in early times to enhance the fertility of the planted crops. It may also have been a remnant of the days when women menstruated in the fields, for the same reason.

Sing

Choose suggested songs for Beltane in the appendix or select songs that have to do with the Goddess, fertility, and celebration.

Chant

> What is the teaching of Beltane? Passion is your birthright.
> Our joy comes from our sensual sexual natures.
> Behold! All acts of pleasure belong to our Goddess.
> We are free to enjoy the mystery of her fertility.
> We seek pleasure and the expression of our passion.
> What is the teaching of Beltane? Be free.

Activity: Weaving with Ribbons of Our Intentions

Have single multicolored ribbons about eight inches long available within a basket on your altar and ask each person to choose a ribbon and think about what it stands for. They can choose words to name their ribbon, such as love, forgiveness, laughter, joy, intelligence, discrimination, growth, etc.

As the leader, you take your ribbon and share its name and then push one end through a small hole or slash that you have made at the center of a large, colorful paper plate. Pull your ribbon through enough so that it is held in place. Say: "My ribbon represents *love* and I add my ribbon to the community."

Pass the plate so that each person can push their ribbon through the center of the plate and say: "My ribbon represents _____ and I add my ribbon to the community."

When all the ribbons are placed through the center of the plate you as the leader can tie them together at the back of the plate. Now you have a bundle of multicolored ribbons streaming from the plate.

Pass the plate around and have each participant weave or braid the ribbons together. Each one can do just a portion of the weaving and then pass it on to the next person. As the plate is passed read the selection below.

Read

> We are a circle. We meet at the center. We are many. We
> are one. We bring our light and our love to share. Our light

grows. We are never-ending. When we create together we make beauty and create peace. And so it is. Blessed be!

Chant

We are the weavers of life.
We are the creators within the grand mystery.
We are the warp. We are the weft.
We are the web. We are the thread.
We are the makers of beauty.
With our hands and our souls and our hearts
We weave and braid and sew our visions.
We are the weavers of life.

Read

This is Beltane, the fullness of spring. It's a time to open and to rise and to grow. May is the time for joy, hope, and promise. We feel excited and the sap of sensuality and sexuality rises in our bodies. The maiden returns from her winter retreat. The young maiden reaches menarche and begins her bleeding. Whether maiden, mother, or crones, all women share this blood mystery with her. And all men, through their association to the women in their lives, are also blessed. We celebrate the blooming of spring and the return of the sun. We plant our food and we plant our dreams and desires. The maiden attracts a lover, the other half of herself, and they learn passions together. All acts of love and pleasure are the rituals of the Goddess. What is it that you wish to attract into your life that is as sweet as honey?

Out of our passions we create. Could this be a baby? Or a project? A piece of art? A poem? Or the trip of a lifetime? What is your joy to celebrate and create today?

Sing

Play music of your choice or sing songs that honor the Goddess.

Guided Meditation

Take your time. Close your eyes and go within. Breathe deeply and slow your breathing down. Let go of the outside world. Drift into peace. Drift into silence. Allow yourself to center at your heart. Focus there and breathe into the silence ... (pause)

You find yourself in a beautiful open field surrounded by a grove of Oak trees. It is warm and inviting and everyone has gathered to celebrate Beltane. Notice the air of anticipation and the beauty of all the women dressed in long flowing dresses with crowns of flowers in their hair. The men have on long white shirts full of decorated embroidered color and sashed at the waist with brightly colored ribbons. There is a table laid out with food and drink. It is a time of great merriment and there is much relief that another hard winter has passed. As you look around you might notice that some of your loved ones are not present, and you remember that they have crossed the veil and you send them some love, as they are not so very far away.

Then the group comes together in a circle. Each person shares what they want to attract into their life. It may be a lover, a new home, a business venture, a child, a piece of art ... (long pause) When it is your turn, share what you would like to attract.

Notice how your circle totally supports you, witnesses your desire, and finds you totally worthy to receive this honey that you want to attract. Take that in and feel that love and support.

Then your group members each take a ribbon that flows from the tall Maypole at the center of your circle. As you stand in pairs, one of you faces right and the other faces left, and the weaving dance of over and under begins. Simply imagine the happy tune of the drum and the fiddle. You hear music and you begin to dance. Imagine the fun and the joy of being in your body and dancing in celebration. As you pass each partner you look into their smiling face with love.

As the dance comes to an end, the Maypole is now woven and the community is restored. Give gratitude for the celebration and for the circle that joined you here. Take a moment to say your goodbyes. Slowly, come back from the grove to your own circle and to the room you began your journey from.

Sharing

Have your participants take a moment to share their experience within the meditation and what they want to attract into their life.

Activity: Jumping the Candle Flame

Have your participants jump the bonfire if you are outside or jump over the flame of a candle if you are inside. (Be cautious with this. Take off long wraps or tuck up long skirts.) This is done for fertility, health, and good luck for the year.

Say: "Before you jump, focus on your wishes so that they may come true. Make your wish out loud as you step over or jump the fire. Make as many wishes as you desire. The last round over the Bel-fire is for good health and prosperity for the year."

Endings

Release the directions and give your gratitude to the energies of Beltane. Open the circle.

TINNE–HOLLY

May 16–June 12
Eighth Lunation, May/June

Ogham: Tinne (tinn-yeh, chin-yuh), T: ⊐

Keywords: Warrior, masculine, direct action, the spear of the warrior or shaman, the art of negotiation, protection, self-surrender for the common good, truth and justice, polarity, duality, balance, legal proceedings, wholeness, relationships

Totems: Swans, the Lovers tarot card, the twins, Castor and Pollux or Polydeuces (Roman and Greek)

Guides and Deities: The warrior, judges, warrior gods and goddesses, the Holly King, Lugh of the light, the underworld goddesses of the dark, Leda and her World Egg (Greek and Roman)

Practical Guidance: Seek balance and be direct. It is time to fight for what is right.

111

Tinne/Holly Month Ceremony

Purpose

Work with conflict and polarity in a relationship. Create a personal wand.

Preparation

Collect enough Holly sticks before your ceremony to give to each of your participants.

Welcome and Greetings

Welcome to out Holly month ceremony. Introduce yourself and go around the circle having each participant share their name and why they came to the circle. Have them close their eyes and share a moment of silence to prepare for the ceremony.

Call the Directions

Call the directions and invoke the energies of the Holly tree (balance, direct action, warrior energy, protection, polarity and wholeness, right relationship) and her totems, guides, and deities (swan). Place Holly leaves and stems on the altar.

Teachings

Holly represents justice and fighting for the underdog. She represents protection.

She also represents polarity, but her main goal is integration and wholeness. Everything today feels more and more polarized. However, the potential is always there for a greater vision and the complement of opposites. Both sides carry truth. How can we include the positives of both and work to heal and bring light to that which is troublesome? How can we bring understanding to that which we reject? This is not compromise but a new potential.

This month also represents lovers and relationships—which also can break down in argument and conflict, each one fighting for who is going to get their way, or out of a desire to be understood or listened to. We seek healing and understanding in our relationships. We build reciprocity and equality within relationships. We seek to build loving and supportive relationships.

Chant

> What is the teaching of the Holly? Justice and fairness.
> Our Holly offers us strength and protection.
> Behold! We stand in our wholeness.
> And we are free to create our relationships in love and understanding.
> We seek healing.
> What is the teaching of the Holly? Unity and diversity.

Guided Meditation

In this journey you will work with an important relationship that is troubling you. You may find yourself coming to a better understanding of the person that you are in a relationship with.

Close your eyes. In your mind's eye, conjure up the person you are in conflict with or have difficulty with. Set the intention to understand this person in a new light. Ask Lugh (the god of light) and the underworld goddesses of the dark to help you with love and understanding. Feel their support and their ability to bring in a new, fresh possibility. Invite in the strength and protection of the Holly.

Use all your inner senses to focus on this person. See them in detail or, if you are not a seer, imagine them, sense them, or simply know ... Slow down to the breathing pattern of this person and breathe with them ...

Remember that so much about conflict has to do with our own projections. When you have an enemy, see if you can claim any of that enemy energy within yourself first. Soon you will begin to receive information. You may understand your own projections and begin to withdraw them from the person or situation... (long pause)

You may realize thoughts, feelings, memories, or messages from this person. These will simply appear. Be willing to just witness this information however it comes to you. Allow compassion and understanding to move from your heart into the person you are connecting to. You may notice your own agenda melting away for this... (long pause)

When you feel complete, pull back into yourself and disconnect from the person. Refocus your attention back onto your own heart. Ground yourself, and when you are ready, open your eyes. (Make sure that each participant has opened their eyes and is fully present within their own body and they have disengaged from the person they were observing.)

Sharing

Pass the talking stick and allow each person to share their experience and ask them to relate how this journey has shifted their perspective of that person and their conflict.

Activity: Dedicating a Holly Wand

Ask each person to choose a Holly stick. They can take this home with them. Ask them to take the time to form it into a wand of protection that will remind them to do their own shadow work (projections onto others or hidden agendas run by unclaimed jealousy, envy, judgment, and wounding) and compassion work—for those they have a difference with, or for themselves when they are engaged in a difficult polarity. Encourage them to embellish their wand when they get home. Go around your circle and have each participant state the intention of what they want their wand to represent. Give them these examples:

- My Holly wand represents forgiveness and understanding.
- My wand represents unity and wholeness.
- My wand will remind me to do my own
  shadow work and claim my own projections.

- My wand represents diversity and respect for difference.
- My wand reminds me to hold the tension between duality and polarity and breathe into a state of neutrality.

Go around the circle and have your participants choose places or situations to send healing energy to. Send healing energy to all those in conflict to help us understand the other side and allow for difference— be it countries, relationships, religions, or belief systems. Have each person point their Holly want to the center of the circle and say "And so it is"

Sing

Choose an ending song such as "May the Circle Be Open," "Merry Meet," or "We Are a Circle" or one that reflects wholeness and unity.

Ending

Give gratitude to the energy of Holly and to the guides and helpers of Holly. Release the directions and open the circle.

A Holly Story: Duality and Wholeness in Relationship

The sign of Gemini (May 21–June 22) and the Holly month (May 16– June 12) share similar themes—both are about duality and holding the tension between opposites. As I think about the sign of Gemini, I also think about Leda and the Swan and the World Egg that held her twins, Castor and Pollux. I think about my own two children and I am reminded of two pieces of art that I created. One was a picture I made right before my son was born in 1981, depicting the World Egg. The other was of two swans, and I made it within a few days of my daughter's birth in 1990.

Duality is represented in my life with the birth of a boy and a girl. My son is a double Gemini, the sign of intimacy (into-me-see). His rising sign and his sun are in Gemini and his life is full of Tinne Holly energy. My daughter was born with her moon in the sign of Sagittarius, which is the sign opposite of Gemini. His sun and her moon are in opposite signs within the zodiac.

These children have their north nodes in opposing signs, hers in Aquarius and his in Leo, and their south nodes in opposing signs, hers in Leo and his in Aquarius. The north node represents what you are moving toward in this lifetime that is new for you. The south node represents lessons learned, skills gained, and what you are moving away from in this lifetime. She is moving away from the need for personal achievement and praise that she already knows quite a bit about. She is moving more toward using her skills to improve the lives of others through progressive avenues. He is moving away from a more universal approach to a more personal one of achievement and recognition. They are teachers for each other, as each holds a key to new growth.

Again, coincidences appear that present opposites: the male and female, the sun and moon, Gemini and Sagittarius, and their opposing nodes in Leo and Aquarius. I am the mama swan, protector and great mother. My children are very different. How am I to parent such opposing personalities?

The pictures I created before the births of my children seem to have everything to do with holding the world of possibilities open and sustained. Holly says: Keep to the wholeness and don't get lost in the details of difference. Honor the wholeness and hold the differences as sacred, not better or less, just perfect in their own way. Hold and honor them in reverence. I am grateful to Holly for her protection and strength, and for this powerful teaching. As with all things, hold the opposites and the magic will unfold. Breathe in neutrality and acceptance.

And it is not just the relationships with my children that Tinne Holly is helpful with. I have my birth sun in the seventh house of relationship and a lot of my will and purpose in this lifetime has been devoted to my relationships, learning about others and still maintaining a relationship with myself. This has been a lifelong process to be sure. I am somewhat embarrassed to say that I have been married many times, but the last one has been for twenty years, thank the Goddess. My friend Cathy said to me something very profound when I was struggling with marriage yet again: "You sure know how to leave a marriage. What you might be struggling with is how to stay in a marriage." That hit a nerve for sure. I do very much want to stay married and be married in a good way. But for me this has been a lifelong challenge. So often I just can't hardly stand the polarity and the conflict.

The Holly reminds me to see things from the larger perspective of the whole. This helps me bring understanding to what I want and to what my partner wants. It helps me to know that there is enough time, energy, and love for both of us in this sacred cauldron called marriage, even when it heats us up and life together feels more like a crucible. It is never either/or. I have the blueprint of the ferocious loyalty and lifelong mating pattern of the swan. When I get lost and discouraged I am reminded to come back to the teachings of Holly and her helpers. This is indeed wise medicine, especially for the relationship challenged like myself.

Holly has everything to do with relationships. And we all know how challenging they can be. Holly can teach us about balance, reciprocity, and maintaining healthy relationships while we also take care of our ourselves. Can you allow the teachings of Holly to remind you that there is enough time, energy, love, and healing for all, yourself included? Can you maintain strong boundaries? Can you remain strong but pliable as the winds of change require flexibility? Can you maintain balance, neither giving in to another's power too much, nor overreacting and fighting for your position all the time? Rest in Holly to help you stay in balance.

Holly also teaches us how to handle polarity. Think about the dualities in your own life. Is it possible for you to bring a sense of neutrality to this set of opposites? Can you embrace the wholeness? If you find yourself feeling that no resolution within a situation or relationship is possible, go sit with a Holly tree. Allow the tree to meld with your energy and to feed you with the energy of wholeness. You will receive exactly what you require in order to deeply understand and appreciate difference. You will understand how important each part is to the whole.

COLL~HAZEL

June 13–July 10
Ninth Lunation, June/July

Ogham: Coll (cull), C: ≣

Keywords: Insight, wisdom, intuition, higher perspective, straight to the Source, fulfillment, bounty, the zenith, abundance, summer, encourage wisdom and vision, divination offers clarity, creativity, grail of innocence, the chalice of love, cauldron of wisdom

Totems: Tortoise, turtles, crustaceans, salmon, scarab, hare

Deities: Merlin, the mother and maiden aspects of the Goddess

Practical Guidance: Practice meditations and follow your inner guidance to find the answers you seek.

Coll/Hazel Month Ceremony

Holiday
The Summer Solstice is June 20/21.

Purpose

Celebrating the Hazel month portal. Connecting with our loved ones that have passed through the veil. Letting go of sorrows so that we can make space to create abundance. Honoring the tears that cleanse us. This is a time to celebrate the waters, and our family connections, and to heal ourselves of our emotional burdens and pains.

Preparation

Cut strips of paper four inches long by a half-inch wide. Make them big enough for participants to write on them, but small enough that they can be burned. Gather enough pencils for your participants to use. Prepare a bowl of hazelnuts. Have an abalone shell or bowl filled with earth to burn messages.

Welcome and Greetings

Welcome to our Hazel month ceremony. Introduce yourself and go around the circle having each participant share their name and why they came to the circle. Have them close their eyes and share a moment of silence to prepare for the ceremony.

Call the Directions

Call the directions and invoke the energies of the Hazel tree (intuition, wisdom, insight, higher perspective, straight to the Source, fulfillment) and her totems, guides, and deities (tortoise and turtles, crustaceans, salmon, scarab, hare, and mother and maiden goddesses). Invite Hazel to lead you to the source within. Ask her to facilitate the flow of your creative energy outward in the world to where it is needed. Hazel opens you to your creativity and insight and she supports poetry, art, song, divination, and the power of meditations.

Sing

Intersperse songs and drumming at times of your choosing. Choose songs that honor the summer and the community.

Teachings

This is the portal of the Coll Hazel month and the Quert Apple month, June 13 to July 10. The totems of this month are all the shelled and protected animals, reminding us to protect that which is vulnerable in our world and in ourselves. These are the crab, the lobster, the tortoise, and the scarab. They teach us to protect and make boundaries for what is most sensitive and vulnerable.

We celebrate abundance, fertility, and power. We invite the fairies to our ceremonies and we are grateful for the beauty of nature. We call in the devas of the wild rose, thyme, and especially heather with her healing.

The hazelnut encourages vision and wisdom, the treasure of wisdom within. It is believed that when the salmon ate the hazelnut he immediately became wise, thus the "Salmon of Wisdom" becomes the symbol for this time of year. We honor our own intuition through our own connection to Source wisdom, guidance, and clarity.

Heralding in the sign of Cancer, we honor compassion, love, family life, and mothering feelings; we think about the past and feel close to friends and family. The moon of this month is called "the cry baby moon." We are close to our tears, and we are invited to honor the cleansing that crying brings. We honor our sorrows and our emotional burdens, but we come together to release these and clear space to create a new story.

We also honor our families and our homes. We honor our mothers and mothering. Our inner sense of esteem and self-worth becomes important to us and we can be protective and defensive if we feel threatened. We honor the "she-bear" part of our nature that will fight to protect her young. We honor our loved ones who have died, as well as our ancestors.

Chant

What is the teaching of the Hazel? Intuition.
Our guidance comes from our heart's connection to source.
Behold! We receive the abundance of summer with gratitude.
And we receive our oracle in the mother's chalice of love.
We seek answers as she whispers in that quiet voice within.
What is the teaching of the Hazel? Wisdom, clarity, and healing.

Guided Meditation

Take a moment to go quietly within and just breathe. Be with the silence for a short time. (Long pause)

Imagine yourself in a meadow encircled by a beautiful grove of trees. All around you are family and friends, as well as those welcomed loved ones and ancestors that have passed on. It is a bright, sunny summer day and you have gathered to celebrate together. Look into the face of each celebrated guest at your own personal gathering. Only those whom you love and trust are allowed. You know that they are your cheerleaders. A huge feast has been prepared and there is a great feeling of excitement and celebration in this reunion. You gather in a circle to dance and sing.

Each gives their own prayer of gratitude for all the bounty and abundance they have received. Take a moment to share your own gratitude with your circle. Take stock of these friends and relatives, and for the lineages that they represent. Feel the blessing and encouragement of those that have crossed the veil but totally support you. Accept their love and support into every cell.

Then let the people at your celebration go around the circle and share with you what they love about you. Listen well and allow their words to pierce you. They are here today to help you let go of your sorrows and burdens, and to encourage you to be proud of your accomplishments. They will help you stand in your power. They are also here today to bring you wisdom.

Thank all those present for their gifts and for their love and support and know that you can return to this celebration anytime you want to just by turning inward and intending to do so. Say your goodbyes and slowly begin to leave your inner world and return to this room and this time. Take the time you need. When you're ready, slowly open your eyes so that I can know that you have returned.

Sharing

Have each of your participants share something from their experience with the meditation.

Activity: Letting Go of Sorrows and Claiming Your Power

Letting go of sorrows: Direct your participants to take a moment to write their sorrows down on prepared strips of paper. Pass around a candle and an abalone shell and have each person burn their papers and have them each say these words: "I give my sorrow to the flames. The Goddess of fire will consume my pain."

After each participant has completed these words, we all respond with "It is done."

Claiming your power: Ask each person to think of something that they are proud of about themselves right now in this moment, or perhaps something they have overcome or are creating. Each person takes a turn and repeats these words:

> "My name is _____.
> I am a powerful person.
> I am powerful now because _____."

After each one speaks, everyone responds:

> "As we say it, so shall it be."

Becoming wise: Pass around a bowl of hazelnuts. Each person should take a nut. Have each person take a moment to close their eyes and go within to imagine becoming the wise salmon. Let them take quiet time to hold that wisdom and to feel that initiation of power and love and truth. Then individually go around the circle. As each person puts the nut in their mouth, everyone responds: "You are wise and loving. All you need to know is alive within your heart."

Sharing

When everyone has consumed their nut, invite each person to share their visions or experiences.

Sing

Choose an ending song that honors the summer and its bounty, or that honors the mother and the maiden aspect of the Goddess.

Endings

Give your gratitude to the energies of the Hazel and her helpers. Release the directions and open the circle.

A Hazel Story: Healing with the Scarab

Have you ever had the experience of forming a question in your mind and then having answers appear for you spontaneously? Before I left for Egypt in October of 2007, my students of Alchemical Healing were asking whether they needed special protection when working with clients that are undergoing chemo or radiation. (Alchemical Healing is a form of energetic healing, created by Nicki Scully and sourced in Egypt, which uses the help of totems, guides, and deities.) My friend and fellow teacher, Danielle Hoffman, said she asked Thoth, our teacher, the ibis-headed god of communication and healing, to build her some special etheric protective gloves when she was first doing the work. This was a good answer, but I was open to knowing more.

On my trip to Egypt I made friends with a wonderful woman who had dealt with cancer more than once and certainly had her share of chemo and radiation. We were together at Khnum's temple at Elephantine Island in the ancient underground sanctuary dedicated to his consort, Satet. For a few magical moments, we were held in bliss and loving ecstasy and were transported to an experience of pure love and healing. I knew I would share further healing with this woman as our trip progressed.

On our boat ride down the Nile, she asked about the scarab god Khepera whose image appears on many temples and tombs in Egypt. I referred her to the chapter on Khepera in Nicki Scully's book, *Shamanic Mysteries of Egypt*. Khepera is the scarab god that represents our becoming. He spins the cycles of life and assists in our transformational processes. He helps us to recognize our god or goddess self so that we can begin to cocreate with spirit the life we desire. Khepera represents the early morning sun, always carrying the promise of what we can become. The scarab is also a totem of the Hazel tree.

In Luxor we finally arranged a healing session and it became very clear that Khepera was to be my new friend's healing ally. She was experiencing discomfort around her neck where she had some suspicious glands removed just before our trip. Khepera wanted to be part of the work and since she had been drawn to him already, she was willing.

Together we entered a shamanic journey, which is another word for pathworking or guided meditation. Khepera is often seen rolling a ball of dung in which its larva is deposited and then safely nourished. In this way the energetic beetle went right to work, entering the places of discomfort in her body. He began rolling up the pain, extra lymph material, scar tissue, inflammation, and any cells that were unnecessary. He worked diligently and gently as he rolled up what no longer served my friend. He pulled out discomfort, infection, and soreness from each node until he was quite content and full, sitting upon the ball of dispensable energies from her neck. He deftly worked with the area that had been disturbed by the surgeon's knife and with the tissues affected by the chemotherapy and radiation.

We filled the places that Khepera had so tenderly worked on with pink light, love, and Universal Life Force energy. And of course, we gave our gratitude to Khepera for his help. When finished, he and his ball dissolved back into the void—what we call Akasha—where all things are created. Thus, this energy can be used to create something new.

Khepera, the scarab beetle, as an insect, is resistant to many of the chemicals and radiation that are harmful to humans, making him a powerful ally for people who are undergoing these treatments. It is not that we are getting rid of the chemo or the radiation, as we want them to do their work. This ally can support whatever protocol you choose and can also help regenerate tissue that is damaged during the treatment.

He also offers protection to me as I do the healing work. Scarab showed me that it is not necessary to handle these toxic energies directly. I do advise great care while working with people with cancer, especially those undergoing radiation therapies. And I do not advise doing Alchemical Healing without training. However, I do want to demonstrate how totems offer themselves for our healing.

After the healing, my friend's neck felt better and the pain decreased. She experienced more range of motion. She also experienced joy, peace, and reassurance. It was quite amazing to participate in this healing and to witness my friend's healing. This is a great example of how totems can share their healing powers and gifts with us.

If you have a body ailment, you can invite in the totems of the trees to assist you. In thinking about the Hazel, we can call in the many helpers. Take a moment to think about how the tortoise, turtles, crustaceans, salmon, scarab, or the hare might help you. It was amazing to me that scarab was just the right totem to assist in this healing. You will be amazed as well by who shows up. This could apply to any physical, emotional, or spiritual challenge. How could Merlin the great wisdom keeper or the mother and maiden aspects of the Goddess assist you? What special insight or wisdom might they offer if you but asked?

If you seek clarity, the actual dryad of Hazel is at your assistance. I invite you to ask for her help. The teaching of the Hazel is to look within and trust your intuition. She asks you to go straight to the source for wisdom, and that doorway to higher dimensions of love and understanding lives within your heart. She invites you to make your decisions based on this heart wisdom. She will not fail you.

QUERT–APPLE

June 13–July 10
Shares with Hazel Month; July/August

Ogham: Quert, Q: ≣|

Keywords: Choice and beauty, Mother Earth, female lineages and ancestral land, apples, pentacle

Totems: The fairies

Guides and Deities: The ancestors, all forms of the Goddess, but especially the mother aspect, Gaia, virgin, lover, and elder

Practical Guidance: Notice and appreciate the beauty around you. You have many lovely choices, but you must focus on only one so that you bring it to manifestation. Feel the amazing wonder of fertility in the paradise called planet earth.

Quert/Apple Month Ceremony

Purpose
To connect to the Apple tree energies. Connecting to the ancestors, making choices, and manifesting our desires

Preparation

You will need apples and to prepare a bowl of seeds. Collect small notebooks and writing materials, enough for each person.

Welcome and Greetings

Welcome to our Apple month ceremony. Introduce yourself and go around the circle having each participant share their name and why they came to the circle. Have them close their eyes and share a moment of silence to prepare for the ceremony.

Call the Directions

Call the directions and invoke the energy of the Apple tree (beauty and choices) and her totems, guides, and deities (the fairies, all goddesses). Take an apple and cut it in half so that the pentagram at the center is visible. Pass this around and have each participant give their gratitude to Mother Earth and thank her for the abundance and nourishment that she has so generously given.

Teachings

The Apple tree is all about bounty, beauty, abundance, and our ancestry. The apple is the fruit of the Great Mother and represents Gaia herself. Thus, the tree ties us to our maternal links, and to the lands from which our ancestors hailed. The tree reminds us that we have many beautiful choices before us as we create the life we want. She reminds us to choose carefully and create beauty. This is a time to invoke Goddess energy for healing and renewal.

Activity: Honoring the Ancestors

Reconnect to your ancestry. Pass the talking stick and have each person tell what countries their ancestors are from. As a group give a moment of silence to honor these ancestors.

Chant

> *What is the teaching of the Apple? Beauty.*
> *Our freedom comes from making choices.*
> *Behold! We are held in the arms of our Great Mother.*
> *And we are free to honor her with our gratitude.*
> *We seek her fulfillment and love.*
> *What is the teaching of the Apple? Manifest your desires.*

Sing

Choose songs that honor the Goddess: mother, maiden, and crone.

Read

Take a moment to consider what stage of life you are in. Remember and honor stages that you have passed through. Review your life as a maiden, mother, and crone. For men this is similar: adolescent, father, and elder ... (long pause)

Review your life choices, blessings, and wrong turns ... (long pause)

Now see yourself fully in the present and look at the road in front of you. Without any sense of restriction, look ahead to what you would like to become and to what you would like to create. Don't allow any excuses or obstacles to inhibit you. Take some time to consider your choices ... (pause) Hold on to these ideas as you enter our journey.

Guided Meditation

Close your eyes and breathe deeply. Allow yourself to let go of the outside world and to drop into a quiet mind. Allow the silence to embrace you. Allow yourself to simply breathe as you rest here ... (long pause)

Imagine yourself on a summer day in a grove of Apple trees. The sun is bright and the sky is blue. There is a gentle breeze and you can smell the blossoms of the trees and hear the buzzing bees as they gather nectar. The birds are chirping above, greeting you as you walk through the grove.

From the edge of the grove emerges the Priestess of Apples. As she walks toward you, you see that she is dressed in a golden gown and she wears a crown of fresh apple blossoms upon her head. She is full of abundance, and has rosy cheeks, lovely red lips, and flowing hair. She walks up to you and greets you with incredible warmth and affection. She holds the most beautiful red apple in her hand.

Still smiling, she reaches down and withdraws a magical amethyst knife from the sash at her waist. She deftly cuts the apple in half and then places the knife back into her sash. She holds both halves in front of you and suggests that you pick a seed. She explains to you that this seed represents a choice. This choice represents your greatest dreams and desires. Without thinking too much you simply choose a seed.

She smiles, very pleased with your choice. She also acknowledges that any choice is a good one. She asks you to dig a little hole and plant your seed into this magical ground. After you have done so, she hands you a little jug of water and suggests that you water your tree.

At that moment, your tree begins to burst through the earth and grow. You take a step back to give your tree the room it needs to grow. Right before your very eyes, your tree begins to grow until it is fully grown.

Take a moment to see your fully grown tree. As you consider this magical apple tree, you see and understand your heart's desire. You may see this as words, or images, or visions. Or you may have a strong sense of knowing about what this tree represents for you. Based upon your choice, your magical apple tree is the symbol for your own longing. Take a moment to really take in the message of your tree … (long pause)

It is time to return to the circle. Give your gratitude to your tree and to the beautiful Priestess of Apples, to her magic and the Apple grove. Return to this room and this place and take a moment to fully ground before you open your eyes.

Sharing

After the journey have your participants share their experiences. What were their seed choices about?

Activity: Apple Seeds, Affirmations, and Apple Slices

Every choice is like a seed. Pass around the bowl of seeds and have each participant take a seed to represent their choice. Ask each one as they pick a seed: "What do you need to do to nurture, protect, and cultivate this choice so that it can be brought forth to manifestation?"

Pass out notecards and pens. Have each person take a moment to write a positive affirmation. Then go around and have each participant read their affirmation out loud.

Pass apple slices and have each person eat one with the intention of moving toward their choice. After each person is complete the group says "And so it is!"

Ending

Give gratitude to the Apple tree and to the Goddess. Release the directions and open the circle.

An Apple Story: The Honoring of Gaia and My British Ancestry

Apple represents our connection to Mother Earth and our connection to our female lineages. We look to the countries from which we hail and we give gratitude to the women who have carried and passed on our DNA. We honor Gaia and we honor our lineages.

While going through a genealogy that my maternal grandfather prepared, I began to really concentrate upon my great-great-great-grandmother. Her name was Mary Jane Penberthy and she was born on the Isle of Man around 1810 or so. I love that she was born on the Isle of Man. From what I have read about this island, it has a strong mystical and magical tradition. Mary Jane Penberthy is one of my important links to the Celtic mysteries that I so love. I love that I have these roots and that I can trace them to a place on earth and to a tangible tradition. I also imagine that it is through this woman's heritage that I have received my sensitivities and my psychic gifts and talents.

I do feel a heartfelt connection with the British Isles, with the elfin people, and with the devas and nature spirits—with the wind and the waves on the shore, with the animals and the stars, with the moon and the sky, and especially with the trees. I get goose bumps just hearing about the likes of fairies, elves, devas, and Druids. I have read: "The fairy-lore of the Isle of Man is only rivaled by the legendary leprechauns of Ireland" and "The fairies were supposed to be the original inhabitants of the Isle of Man, and everything was carried on in a supernatural manner" (Leek 1976, 24, 26). It is also said that it was this mystical climate that lured the Druids to the Isle of Man for refuge. The Manx people (those that hail from the Isle of Man) have a rich tradition of stories, legends, and superstitions, and today there are still those who follow the old nature and folk religions.

I am fascinated by one of their famous goddesses and prophetesses I have read about that comes from this area. She is called Caillagh-nyp Ghueshag. She had the power to transport herself anywhere she desired. She could also shape-shift her physical appearance at will. She might appear as the old crone or hag known as the Cailleach, or she might choose the form of the youthful maiden. She is revered for her knowledge of herbs and her ability to heal. Overall, she chose to use her powers fairly and for the benefit of others. I find this witch-heroine figure fascinating. In fact, the name Rhiannon comes from the Welsh version of this same mythical Goddess. It is a version of this name that I have chosen for my daughter Rianna to honor my father's family, which hails from Wales.

The indigenous people of the British Isles followed a native spirituality that we can only speculate about. However, it is known that these ancients had a belief and reverence for nature and the earth and they considered her a living entity. They worshiped nature spirits much like the Native American peoples of this continent do. I refer to them as the nature peoples or the native Europeans. They understood nature and worked closely with the healing aspects of herbs, plants, and trees.

It is true, however, that the spirituality of these people came under siege through the invasion of various groups over time—by the Roman occupation, through the Catholic Inquisition and the Protestant witch hunts. Many call the period of European religious inquisition a hysterical holocaust for the nature peoples and especially women. In these times many were labeled as witches and said to be controlled by Satan. Yet this terror was used to gain people's lands and resources and destroy their beliefs and indigenous wisdom. It was a successful means of gaining control by the church and the governments of the time.

I've read that it was Henry VIII who made a formal proclamation that witches should be dispensed with in the British Isles. On the Isle of Man, women who were accused of witchcraft were thrown into bogs; if they sank, they were declared innocent and given a decent Christian burial. Big deal. If they were indeed witches, they swam to dry land. After their little swim, they were treated to an assortment of diabolical ways in which they would be murdered. I think if anyone was associating with evil and consorting with Satan, it was those legal women-killers.

There is a famous bog on the island called Curragh Class, which is associated with these murders. I should like to see that bog someday. I would like to say a prayer over that place and honor all the women who were murdered for practicing a way of life that the church wanted to wipe out. I wish I had visited it when I was in England in 1973, but I didn't even get to the island. How was I to know that it was going to become an important place to me, a very important place?

I am grateful to my great-great-great-grandmother. Although, come to think of it I could also be grateful to the man she married, Samuel James Cornelius. He was born in Cornwall and they say that Cornwall is one of the few places left that is holding on to its Celtic traditions. Maybe my Celtic heart came through my great-great-great-grandfather. Who's to say? To be exact, I could say that I am grateful for their union. I am beholden to my mother's and my father's ancestry.

When I used to work as a mental health therapist at Catholic Community Services, my clients often asked me if I was Catholic. I always wondered what they would do if I replied, "Well no, actually I am a Buddhist Pagan witch tree lady!" I used to feel that my sensibilities and leanings were weird and strange, especially for someone who was "born again" at the age of nine and raised Methodist. (I have heard that the word *weird* comes from the word *wyrrd*, which refers to the study of power and magic in ancient Europe. How many times do you hear people say, "It was really weird," when something strange and unexplainable happens?)

But coming into a greater knowledge of my heritage provides me with a different sense of who I am. I am proud to claim a tradition that honors and reveres the mysteries of nature and respects the Great Mother known as Gaia. Today we have what is called Wicca or "the craft of the wise." Many are proud to call themselves Pagans, witches, Goddess worshippers, or medicine women. Whatever we call ourselves, I am glad to know that I can claim a tradition that lived well upon the planet for so long and still thrives today. I am honored to find inspiration in a way of being upon the planet that honors nature and seeks to protect and preserve it and all its life forms.

The Apple tree reminds you to send some love to your ancestors and to the women in your family. Give gratitude to what your mother was able to give you or teach you. And if you have regrets or resentments, thank her—she was your backwards teacher. You learned from her what you do not want to do. Do the same for your father. Gratitude and forgiveness are the best medicine. Bring in Apple blossoms to remind yourself that the earth is a bountiful paradise. Can you commit to be the best steward you can be? Think about ways to support the earth and ensure clean water and air. Remember that the air that we breathe comes from the trees—they are the lungs of our planet.

Because the element of water is tied to the sign of Cancer and this time of year, it is a time to really consider the waters of the planet. It is important to honor the water on the planet, and so we are reminded to be grateful for this gift, and to work toward restoring all the water to purity. This is a precious resource, and she requires our protection. If possible, I encourage you to find one thing that you can do to help with this.

Find out more about your own ancestry and the lands that your family has hailed from. Also research the spiritual lineages that you are attracted to. Many people feel drawn to the British Isles, but often Egypt and Peru as well. What is your special place that makes you feel closer to your most authentic self and your own spiritual identity?

And finally, in contemplating the Apple tree, give gratitude for the abundance in your life that she represents, as well as the mystery and magic of that energy and vibration that lives just beyond this world. She represents the many beautiful choices that you have and your ability to create the reality that you want to live in—moment to moment through your choices. Choose beauty. Choose peace. Choose kindness.

Summer Solstice Ceremony
June 20/21

The Summer Solstice marks the zenith of the sun's power in the Northern Hemisphere. We celebrate summer and the fullness of Mother Earth's abundance that she shares with us. We celebrate fertility: the magic of pregnancy, progeny, and growth, and the fulfillment of the flowers, the fruits of the trees, and the magic manifestation of the vegetables, legumes, and grains that sustain us and all of life on our planet. This is a time to count our blessings and give our gratitude. Another name is Litha.

Purpose

To celebrate the solstice.

Preparation

Cut some heather and bring it in for your altar. Alternately, buy a heather plant and place it in a beautiful pot. Gather rose petals in a bowl. Place a large, beautiful container of water at the center of your circle. Find a staff or scepter that you can use for the ceremony. You can also use a wand.

Welcome and Greetings

Welcome to our Summer Solstice ceremony. Introduce yourself and go around the circle having each participant share their name and why they came to the circle. Have them close their eyes and share a moment of silence to prepare for the ceremony.

Call the Directions

Call in the directions and the energies of the Summer Solstice.

Teaching

Since the Winter Solstice, the shortest day of the year, the sun has been inching its way back into our lives. Rising slightly earlier each morning and setting a minute or two later every night, it graces us with light gradually gained. The change is at first imperceptibly slow, but it is steady, and soon the minute-by-minute accumulation of daylight asserts itself in more and more hours of summer. The Summer Solstice is the high point of the year's outward expansion of growth in northern countries. Other names for this solstice are Alban Heruin, Midsummer's Eve, and Litha. Where the Winter Solstice celebrates the births of the sons of great mothers, the Summer Solstice celebrates the mother herself in her fullness.

We honor our strengths, gather together outside, and celebrate the beauty of the green world.

We celebrate abundance, fertility, and the full power of the sun. We invite the fairies and elfin people to our ceremonies and we are grateful to the beauty of nature. The Hazel tree and Apple tree are honored this month. We call forth the devas of wild rose, thyme, and heather as well.

In summer, joy and blessings abound. Everything in nature is growing, flowing, and blossoming. The fruits are sweet, fat, and deliciously juicy. The vegetable gardens are ripe for picking and vacation days come none too soon. Summer is the season of the longest day, yet the longest day also begins the decline of the sun's power, heralding in the onset of autumn. And again, the wheel takes another turn.

Sing

Choose songs of gratitude for the earth and for the Goddess.

Chant

> *What is the teaching of the Summer Solstice? Bounty and abundance.*
> *Our freedom comes from dancing and singing.*
> *Behold! The mother Goddess blesses us with her fullness*
> *And we are free to express our joy and happiness.*
> *We seek to celebrate with our loved ones.*
> *What is the teaching of the Summer Solstice? Gratitude.*

Read

> Behold, it is summer!
> Our Mother Earth in her fullness
> blesses us with her abundance.
> She offers her fruitfulness.
> And we give her our gratitude and
> we are full of thanks giving.
> Behold it is the Summer Solstice!
> Our Mother Earth in her fertility
> honors us with her bounty
> She offers her blessings
> And we give her our gratitude
> and we are full of thanks giving.
> Behold it is the growing season!
> Our Mother Earth in her fullness
> shares with us her growing fields
> She offers us life.
> And we give her our gratitude
> and we are full of thanks giving

Guided Meditation

Close your eyes and turn your attention to your breath. Slow your breath down and focus on your heart. Send some love to your heart and continue to breathe slowly. Let go of your busy life and all its needs and wants. Simply let go and be in this quiet moment.

Imagine that you can safely travel to the sun... (pause) When you arrive, you find that you can merge safely with the sun. As you enter its heat and light and power you are fully protected. Simply step into the heart of the sun and merge with its brilliance...

Notice what you notice. Take in its intense power. Let it fill you with its life-giving light. You find that you *are* the sun, and you experience its fullness and its dazzling light. You know that you are one with the infinite sun, forever, and ever, and ever... (long pause)

When you are ready, step out of the sun and give it your gratitude for all that it does for life on our planet. Appreciate it and allow its potential to fill you with hope and new life. Let it grow you and move you toward your possibilities. Know too that you have a destiny to fulfill, as you are an important part of the cosmos and you have the same creative dynamic within your own cells as the sun does in its cells. You can become like the sun within your own life. (Pause)

It is time to return from your journey. When you are present, open your eyes, ground, and center.

Sharing

Pass around the talking stick and let the group share their experiences from the meditation.

Song

Choose songs that honor the sun and the fullness of summer.

Chant

> *The sun is our light and our warmth*
> *and our life, forever, and ever, and ever.*

Activity: Activating the Power of the King and Queen Archetype

The solstice marks the zenith of the sun's power. Our human representative of the fullness of the sun is the king or queen archetype. This is also represented by our heroes and heroines. Who in your life has impacted you the most? Allow each person to respond.

Take a moment to become a great king or queen. What would you wish for the world? Take on the role of the king or queen and speak your proclamations! Give them a scepter and pass it around so that each person can make their proclamations. For instance, "I proclaim that there is no more war!" Pass the scepter around many times, as this is quite a lot of fun.

Read

Here tonight we find courage, intellectual competence, and self-confidence.

We embrace light and clarity. Here we meet our fears and let them go and treat them with kindness, but we do not give our power over to them. It is a good time for positive energy, for making resolutions and vows that require inner strength. Close your eyes and think about your aspirations. Who do you aspire to be? (Pause)

Take a moment to contemplate a symbol that can represent your aspiration … (pause) For instance, the scarab is a symbol representing the process of our becoming. Who are you becoming?

Sharing

Have your participants share their aspirations and the symbol that they chose to represent that aspiration. Have them also state what they are becoming.

Read

We invoke you our Cosmic Mother.
We invite you to our circle.
We see you all around us.
You are here in the buzzing bees of summer.
You are here in the array of colors and aromas of the flowers.
You are here in the growing of the vegetables in our gardens.
You are here in the babbling brook.
You are here in the bright azul sky above.
You are here as the sun shines warm upon our day.
You are here in the wispy clouds that dance across the horizon.
And we are grateful.
As you have created a paradise for us.
They say that this is a good time to make a wish.
May we ask of you our heart's desire?

May you grant us the fulfillment of this wish.
May you hear our prayers for peace.
May you offer your guidance.
May you extend your blessing for our health.
And for the fulfillment of our holy purpose.
Thank you for offering us such bounty.
Such beauty and such brilliance.
May we learn to share as you do.
May we learn to be compassionate as you are.
May we grow to hold the sacred and protect you.
May we give back to you.
And never take you for granted.
Our hearts are filled with love.

Activity: Rose Petals and Wishes

Summer Solstice is a magical time for wishing and for sending a message to the Cosmic Mother, whose symbol is the rose. Pass around a bowl of rose petals and ask each person to choose a petal. Each one sends their wishes out into the world by kissing their rose petal, giving their gratitude to the Cosmic Mother, and placing it into the bowl of water at the center of the circle. The participants can say their wishes out loud or keep silent as they kiss their petal.

Read

May we be aligned with you our Great Mother, so that your powers may flow through us and be expressed by us for the good of this planet Earth and for all living beings upon it. We gladly welcome and accept joy, prosperity, and goodness with gratitude, through people, places, things, and situations that bless us. And so it is!

Ending

Release the directions with gratitude for the fullness of summer and for all the blessings and open the circle.

MUIN–VINE & BRAMBLE
July 11–August 7
Tenth Lunation, July/August

Ogham: Muin (muhn), M: ᚋ

Keywords: Harvest, fruits of one's labor, prophecy, the clan or community, the results of the sacred marriage, gratitude and celebration

Totems: Lion, the fairies, sylphs, nymphs, elves

Guides and Deities: The sun god, Lugh; the mother aspect of the Goddess; the Green Man; Modron, the Mother of All; Madron, the white horned, red-eared cow goddess in Britain; the Deae Matronae; the Triple Goddess; Sun Goddesses—Greine (Scotland), Griane (Ireland), Ker, the grain Goddess (Britain)

Practical Guidance: Speak up. You have a voice. Now is the time.

Muin/Vine Month Ceremony

Holiday

Lammas is August 1.

Purpose

Honoring the mother, fertility, and abundance. To celebrate the portal of the Vine. To encourage you to be yourself boldly, receive recognition, and celebrate yourself as the god or goddess that you truly are.

Preparation

Gather vines and brambles for your altar, and prepare bowls of grapes, blackberries, and raspberries for your group to sample.

Welcome and Greetings

Welcome to our Vine month ceremony. Introduce yourself and go around the circle having each participant share their name and why they came to the circle. Have them close their eyes and share a moment of silence to prepare for the ceremony.

Call the Directions

Call in the directions and invoke the energies of the Vine (harvest, fruits of one's labor, prophecy, the clan or community, the completion, gratitude, and celebration) and her totems, guides, and deities (lions, the Green Man, Lugh, the fairies). Call forward the representatives of the mother. For example, "We call Gaia, Mother Mary, Isis (Egypt), Kuan Yin (China), Tara (Tibet), and other such figures." Go around the circle and have each participant say their own name including their maiden name. For instance, "My name is Sharlyn [middle, maiden, married name]." Then have each participant state their mother's full name as well.

Teachings

With the Vine portal we celebrate the first fruits and grains harvested from the growing season. We celebrate. We celebrate summer and we celebrate our families and children. We celebrate all that we have created. This is a portal in which we give our gratitude to Gaia for all that she provides for us. We celebrate the full sun.

We also honor our own magnificence and choose to view ourselves as the gods or goddesses that we truly are. We honor our power and the gift of our will and intention to create our reality. We review why we are here, what gifts we have been given, and what it is that we are destined to do in this lifetime. The Vine asks us to be ourselves boldly in the world. Once we sacrifice our smaller ego-interested self in favor of our larger loving, unlimited, and wise spiritual self, we are truly unstoppable.

Read

Today we honor you as king/god or queen/goddess for a day. It is your day to be yourself boldly. And it is a day to receive praise, applause, and recognition.

Close your eyes for a moment and imagine yourself as a queen or king sitting on a throne with a lion, leopard, jaguar, or cougar companion. These large felines represent the power to use your own will to go after your dreams and desires. Merge with your lion friend and feel that determination and ferocity. Claim these as your own. Imagine the power of the full summer sun running through your veins. Imagine that in the true Leo fashion you accept your powers and your dominion over your realm. Be willing to drop any judgment about this. Simply claim your throne. (Long pause)

(Invite them to open their eyes.)

It is said that we are indeed gods and goddesses housed in physical bodies and that we hail from the stars. For a moment imagine that you are indeed a shining star and that you embody all potential and possibility. It is said that it is a privilege to be born into this dimension and that once we wake up to the fact that we can cocreate with spirit, we can claim our own amazing power and potential as living kings and queens, gods and goddesses. Once we claim this spiritual power we are less interested in meeting the needs of our ego selves, and more interested in helping others and raising consciousness and awareness. We claim our true purpose, which is to be responsible stewards of our planet and to turn our base essence into gold. It is from this higher perspective and potential that we can create miracles.

Activity: Self-Recognition

Pass the talking stick around and ask each participant to "brag" about themselves. This is an opportunity to stand in the limelight and receive. This can be about inner work, outer accomplishment, or anything they are proud of themselves about. One can also claim their own special gifts. I might brag about my artwork, my writing, the class I taught, or that special dinner I made. I might mention my creativity and ability to dream. When each person is finished, the group says together:

> We honor you and recognize you for all you are and all you do.
> We see that you are the king or queen of your own life.
> We honor the god or goddess that you are.

Then they are celebrated with a round of applause. Give each person a moment to receive this recognition.

Sing

Choose songs that celebrate the sun and community.

Chant

> What is the teaching of the Vine? Speak your truth.
> Our freedom comes from understanding our magnificence.
> Behold! We are gods and goddesses
> And we are free to become shining stars.
> We seek our birthright and give our gratitude to our star ancestors.
> What is the teaching of the Vine? Claim your power.

Guided Meditation

Close your eyes and place your attention on your breath. Take some long, slow, and deep breaths. Allow yourself to slow down and enter a moment of silence. Focus on your heart and send yourself a blast of love and care. Find a moment of peace here as we enter our journey ... (pause)

Imagine yourself standing on a green, grassy hill. It is summer and below you a vast valley stretches out as far as the eye can see. You allow the heat of the sun to enter every cell of your being. You absorb the heat and luxuriate in the calm, bright summer day. You take in the view of the valley of grapevine fields below you. Each vine is carefully resting upon its own tau-cross, which supports its growth. You smell the sweetness of the grapes ripening on the vines.

Wine is said to be the drink of the gods and goddesses. It is said to bring truth. It is the nectar of ecstasy. You notice that you hold in your hand a cup of the loveliest wine. If you don't like alcohol, notice that your cup holds grape juice. This nectar is ambrosia to you and it is magical. You can smell its sweet bouquet and imagine its citric flavors and spices.

Take a sip of the beautiful, smooth, and crisp drink and feel it as it moves down your throat. Allow it to transform your perspective. You see all the bounty upon the earth and you feel such incredible gratitude for all the amazing gifts of Gaia.

You understand too that as a member of the human species you can move around, unlike the plant kingdom. The plant world often needs you to care for it. This is part of our stewardship. You can see the many people on earth that work carefully to plant and produce food. Feel your gratitude.

You also feel the gratitude that you have for your own bounty and abundance. You too are a flower that has so much to offer the world. You can feel the appreciation for the blessings that life has in store for you. You are totally supported as you blossom and share your gifts with the world. Take that in for a moment. Really allow it in. Vine's message to you today is that you are already a god or goddess, and that you are a part of the cornucopia of magnificence.

As you look about the valley of abundance, you understand just how much you are a part of nature, and just how valuable you are. You are the fruit of your parents and you hold the aspirations of your ancestors. This is a day of great celebration. This is a day to celebrate you and to take your own aspirations and ambitions seriously. No second guessing, no putting yourself down, and no excuses. See yourself as the god or goddess that you are and see the sun's light filling you with all the energy and knowing that you need to accomplish your own goals ... (long pause)

Give your gratitude to the drink of truth, to the grapevines, to the valley of abundance and to the paradise that you live in. Feel the grace of being such an important species and think of how you can help to take care of the mother. Mostly she would love gratitude and appreciation, so send her your energy and shine your light upon her. Give gratitude to the Vine for her teachings.

As you return from the journey, take a moment to ground and center. Take a moment to become very quiet and still and pay attention to your breath. Allow yourself to slow down, to drop down, to slow your breath, and to take deep breaths. Just be with that for a moment. When you are ready, open your eyes and record your experience in your journal.

Sharing

Allow the group time to share their experiences with Vine. Pass around the talking stick and have each participant share what they are most grateful for. Also have them share what they are bringing into fruition, and their aspirations.

Sing

Choose songs that honor the mother aspect of the Goddess or simply drum and tone together. You will find that when you open yourself up the energies that flow through you express the abundance of this time of year. Have fun and lose yourself in the music.

Activity: Laughter, Dancing, Silence, and Toasting

If people have funny stories or jokes to share this is a great time to laugh together. Put on some lively music and dance together, or if someone knows a folk dance have them teach the dance to your group. Hold hands and dance in a circle.

When this portion of the ritual is complete, take a moment of silence together. Pass out a small glass of wine or juice to your participants and make a toast to the mother aspect of the Goddess and to her fertility. Toast all her helpers—especially the fairies and the nymphs of the forest. Toast your gratitude to the abundant cornucopia of the fruits, vegetables, and grains of the season. Toast the sun for its life-giving rays and energy. Finally, toast each person in the group and recognize them as the gods and goddesses that they truly are.

Ending

Give your gratitude to the Vine, and to the totems, guides, and deities. With gratitude, release the directions and open the circle.

A Vine Story: Communications from My Parents on the Other Side

I was conceived on August 1, 1946—my parents' wedding anniversary. This date was written upon the back of a photo of my parents; my mom was twenty-eight and my dad was thirty-two. They sat on the grass in front of a rustic fishing lodge. They were on a summer getaway, to have some time for themselves and to have a break from parenting their three children. My mom was draped in a bear skin. Little did she know that she was soon to become the mother bear of her fourth child.

It seems appropriate that I celebrate this date. I am sure that they had no idea about the significance of this date for Pagans. Lammas, or August 1, is the holiday that celebrates the sacred marriage and the insemination of the seed that is carried in the womb of the Great Mother—so that new life can burst forth in the springtime of the next year's cycle. And I am one of those May babies! This is the good news. I am the fruit of my parents' union!

Unfortunately, August is also the time of year that I am reminded of my mom's death. She died in 1985, just a couple of days before her forty-fifth wedding anniversary. She died of an accidental drowning.

After my mother's death, I had a series of dreams and synchronicities in which I felt that my mother was contacting me. There is one dream about my mother that particularly haunted me. In the dream I find my mother's large wooden Chinese chest with the carvings of dragons and cherry trees that had belonged to my grandmother. It was in an antique store in Bellingham, Washington. As I opened the top of the chest there were many of her things still there in the shallow, large drawer that sat upon the other contents of clothing underneath ... it held jewelry, little trinkets, little purses, rings in special boxes, and keys.

I was surprised, within the dream, to see these same little things that I used to look at when I was a child and Mom wasn't home, although they were in a little dressing table's drawer, not her Chinese chest. I used to love to look at these and wonder what they meant to her. Being that my mom was somewhat distant, this was one way that I connected with her and wondered about her past and why she treasured these little mementos. The dream brought me close to my mother in a most familiar way.

And then within a few days I experienced another synchronicity. I went to the Quaker's Friend Center here in Seattle. When I walked into the bathroom there was a dressing table/desk there just like the one my mom used to have. In fact, it was my mom's! It was the one in which all her personal little mementos were stored. The same momentos I saw in the dream, and the same ones I used to look at when I was a child!

As for the dressing table, everything was the same, down to the nail holes that she used in the little arms to make them move out to the right and left so she could get to the drawers to open them up. It had also once held fabric that skirted in front of the desk when the arms closed. There was a glass top and a little slanted board for one's feet at the bottom. The burn marks on the back of the desk from a heater were there. My mom must have given this table to Goodwill or some other charitable organization and it eventually made its way to the Center.

There was something powerful and satisfying in touching the little table. It was like contacting my mom. I could distinctly remember the many little keepsakes once nestled in its drawers. It was the strangest coincidence and I had such a powerful feeling of déjà vu. While standing there remembering my mom, my mind went to how my mom died—her accidental drowning.

The thought of her death made me sad. I miss her. I wished I could honor her and thank her for being my mother. And I wished I could feel, in the real-life way, her presence, with all her weaknesses and failings, and all her strengths, gifts, and talents. And I wondered about these synchronistic experiences with my dream and then finding her actual dressing table. I knew there was a communication going on—even though her spirit was no longer embodied.

A couple of years later another strange thing happened regarding this original dream and my mom. My friend Barbara called me and told me that she had picked up two of my mother's paintings at a Salvation Army store in Everett, which is about an hour north of Seattle. Barb restores old paintings and she's forever browsing in secondhand stores. Now she shouldn't have known that these were my mom's paintings except that she and her husband had come to an open house of mine just the weekend before and she had seen some of my mom's other paintings. The frames are quite unique because my mom made them.

It was all such a weird coincidence. One painting was a portrait of a Hawaiian woman and the other was of my sister sitting and reading in a rocking chair when she was about thirteen. What made this so poignant was that my mother created a matching pair of paintings on a series of rainy summer days at our beach cabin—one of me facing to the left while sitting in one of our rocking chairs, and one of my sister, facing right, sitting in the other. I think I was around eight. Mom always displayed these paintings together. When she died, I got mine, and my sister got hers plus the Hawaiian painting. My sister must have given them away when she moved from Washington to California. Now I display them both together. Apparently Mom wanted these to stay in the family!

The interesting thing is that just last year my niece, Karin, told me that Mom has become her spirit guide. Karin had come to this while working with a healer. I was sort of surprised because I thought Mom might not be such a great guide. Karin told me that Mom expected that response, but asked Karin to pass on to me the message that she is no longer in the state of limitation she was in when she was incarnated as my mother.

So, although Mom isn't in a body, she does seem to be very connected to me and Karin. She has been able to communicate with me through synchronicities and dreams and other people and the many secondhand stores in the area! I am glad for her love.

I would be remiss if I left out the communication I received from my father. He died of esophageal cancer in 1995. I had a rather startling visitation from him when I was in Egypt in 2014, and my brother was with me. We were in the Valley of the Kings in the tomb of Siptah where we usually have some private time. Here we honor our ancestors and our loved ones who have passed on. The tomb is full of the ancient artwork that describes the death process the ancient Egyptians seemed to understand. They saw death as an opening to greater light. One feels uplifted and reassured there.

We had a lovely and moving ceremony, and as we were leaving I heard a clear message from my father. He said, "Tell your brother that he did nothing wrong. Tell him that he took care of my dying and my pain with exquisite sensitivity and I am grateful." As soon as we ducked out of the entrance back into the light I told my brother and we both just burst into tears.

Although my brother knew that he had done the right thing, he had felt some guilt, as our stepmother had accused him of killing my dad—which was never true. She was just in that crazed grief place. My brother, as a physician's assistant, had assisted my father with his pain during the last stages of cancer.

That is the last thing I would have imagined happening—in a tomb, in the Valley of the Kings, in Egypt, and with my brother. Our dead do want to communicate with us! I am glad that in such a place, where the veil is indeed thin, my father was able to communicate to my brother how grateful he was. That was a most healing experience.

So, the Muin month always reminds me to give my gratitude for my parents' union. I think of my conception and her death in August. I am happy to hold on to her paintings, although I have given a few to my nieces, Karin and Sarah. The painting of the Hawaiian woman's face went to my daughter, Rianna. These girls are the continuing fruit of my family and I honor them, especially at this time. We indeed are the fruits of our ancestors and I am glad to honor my ancestors by passing their things down to the next generation in my family. And I will take this opportunity to give my love and gratitude to my mom, Marjorie, and my dad, William Ross.

Our dead loved ones, our ancestors, our lineages, and our places on earth are all part of the mystery that lead us to valuable change, forgiveness, and healing. Keep an open mind and an open heart. You can receive loving messages as well.

This portal of the Muin/Vine is a wonderful time to write down your memories of your loved ones that have passed on. It is a great time for family reunions and sharing stories of our ancestors and loved ones. This will draw them close. You too may be visited by a loved one who has passed on to the other side. They hear us and care about us. It is worth thinking about them and remembering the good times. They stay alive when we honor them. They appreciate our remembering them. They do try to contact us, and they do offer us love and support if we are open.

Think about what you are creating that you are leaving to the younger generation. It is a time of gratitude and remembering. Take the opportunity during this period to stop and reflect and count your own blessings, and the blessings of those who have gone before you. You are carried on their shoulders; their mistakes as well as their triumphs move through you in your dreams and aspirations. Vine reminds us that we are indeed the fruits of our ancestors. We are asked to live to our fullest potential and also to support and encourage those who come after us.

Lammas/Lughnasa/Lughnassad Ceremony
August 1

Lammas celebrates the first fruits of the harvest. This is the time in Celtic traditions when marriages took place, legal proceedings were dealt with, and contests and sporting events occurred. This was a time of gratitude for the abundance of the season.

Preparation

Make or buy some biscuits or bread to represent the sun god Lugh. Supply paper cups with plastic tops, Magic Markers to decorate the cups, and a large amount of seeds to place in the cups. Gather an ear of corn and a stalk of grain.

Welcome and Greetings

Welcome to our Lammas ceremony. Introduce yourself and go around the circle having each participant share their name and why they came to the circle. Have them close their eyes and share a moment of silence to prepare for the ceremony.

Call the Directions

Call in the directions and the energies of Lammas.

Teachings

This celebration occurs on August Eve and it called Lammas, the Feast of the Bread, Lughnassad, or Lughnasa. This is a celebration of gratitude. We are grateful for the harvest, feasting, and general merriment. We celebrate agriculture. We celebrate the holy union of the Great Goddess and the Great God represented by Ker and Herne the Hunter (who becomes the great horned stag god Cernunnos—the son/stag/god/hunter). Whether we are talking about the sacrifice of the deer or the sacrifice of the god Lug or Lud or Lugh, the vegetation deity, we are giving gratitude for that which has been sacrificed (reaped) and buried (composted) to ensure life. Every part of that which was sacrificed was a gift to the mother to renew and replenish the soil—we are talking about death as a means of supporting life. We are grateful for the sacrifice. Gratitude is imperative.

This is also a time when we honor the sun god of light, Lugh. Thus, the fullness of summer and the zenith of the sun are celebrated, as represented by the astrological sign Leo. This light enters our body through the food that we consume. We honor all those that are involved in the planting, reaping, and production of our food, as well as the hunters and gatherers. We honor the food, we honor the animals, we honor the four elements and open to the power and vibration of spirit, light, and unity consciousness. We allow the love to fill us and remind us of our true nature, which is not of time or place but is everywhere and everything simultaneously.

The seeds that are gathered will be stored so that they can be planted in the spring, so that the vegetation god can rise again from the dead as a new crop cycle. Babies conceived on August 1 are born at Beltane, which is May 1, and they represent the light of hope and renewal that spring promises. And so, the cycle of life is ensured.

Sing

Choose songs that celebrate abundance, summer, and the harvest.

Chant

What is the teaching of Lammas? Gratitude.
Our lives depend upon her bounty.
Behold! The mother feeds us and she cares for us.
In turn we care for the flora and fauna that share our world.
We seek to be her worthy stewards and guardians.
What is the teaching of Lammas? The earth is sacred.

Guided Meditation

Close your eyes and go within. Take some time to rest here as you slow down and focus on your breath. Take some deep breaths. Let yourself relax. Sit in this quiet space for a brief time ... (pause)

Allow yourself to travel beyond the borders of the world to outer space. Know that you are fully protected as you view the little spinning blue ball that we call Earth. See her in all her splendor and think about how perfect she is. See her absolute beauty. From this perspective, all your troubles and thoughts fade away, and you see the intense perfection of life on planet Earth.

As you return to your home planet you find yourself in a clearing within a forest. You see all kinds of trees and plant life, as well as the little creatures and birds that live here. You see a profusion of life. You see and smell the colorful flowers and you hear the buzzing bees as they gather their nectar. Above you, you see the sun, the blue sky, and the rolling clouds.

You begin to understand how all this profusion fits together to support life, and how the mystery reveals itself in this profusion. You experience how blessed you are to be part of this story. You feel a deep sense of responsibility for stewarding this life and for protecting it. You feel a deep gratitude for this life that sustains you. You know that it is your responsibility to honor life as sacred and protect your planet in her purity—her water, her soil, her air, and her great heart that shares so bountifully. You deeply feel gratitude. And she is happy to receive your gratitude. Take a moment to commune with Gaia and thank her ...

When you feel complete you may slowly begin to return. You can return to this forest clearing anytime you want to. You will be reminded that you live in a paradise. When you are ready, open your eyes.

Sharing

Have your participants share experiences from the meditations.

Activity: A Bread Blessing

Pass around the bread that you have prepared and have each participant take a piece or pull off a small piece if the bread is whole.

Read

Bread is symbolically eaten as we internalize the light of the vegetation, the grain that feeds us. The grain or the corn symbolizes the holy mystery that as both seed and edible fruit, we feed our bodies and allow for a new season of growth and life. Thus, the virgin and maiden aspect of the Goddess represents the child of the earth, the fruits of the first harvest. The mother is the life-giving aspect and holy magic that manifests the fruit. The crone is the withered plant gone to seed ready to rest in the underworld to be resurrected in the spring.

Have them eat their bread and repeat after you: "We celebrate this nature magic today. We absorb this mystery and this renewal. By eating this bread, we eat the light of our sun and we acknowledge our own power. We give our gratitude to our Mother Earth for all she supplies us. We promise to create beauty just as she does. We promise to shine like our sun. We give our gratitude for this first harvest and for this life. And so it is."

Activity: Making a Seed Rattle

Say: "This is a time of gratitude and so we honor the seeds that we gather that are provided so lovingly by Gaia, our Mother Earth. We will use these seeds to create our own power implements. We will make rattles to add to our ceremonies when we sing and drum. A rattle can call in the spirits. They are attracted to the sound. You can make the rattle part of your own music. And the rattles will remind us to be grateful every time we use them."

Each person is given a cup, a handful of seeds, and a pop-on lid. They can decorate their cup with Magic Markers. Then they can place a handful of seeds within it and pop on the top. When everyone is finished, have your group make sounds together with their new rattles.

Sharing

Go around the circle and have each participant shake their rattle to their own beat. Have them share what they are grateful for and what has come to fruition in their lives.

Activity: Making a Corn and Grain Prayer

Pass around the ear of corn and a stalk of grain. Have each person contemplate the mystery here. As they hold the corn and grain have each person make a prayer for the earth.

Sing

Choose a song that honors the Great Goddess, summer, the mother aspect of the Goddess, gratitude, and thanksgiving.

Sharing

Share ideas of how we can care for the earth in our own lives.

Ending

Release the directions with gratitude and place people, situations, and events into the circle for healing. Open the circle.

GORT–IVY

August 8–September 4
Eleventh Lunation, August/September

Ogham: Gort (gor'it), G: ⟨symbol⟩

Keywords: The labyrinth, inner knowing, the journey into the self, the spiral, the double helix, the DNA

Totems: Spider, wolf

Guides and Deities: The weaver aspect of the Goddess, Spider Woman (Native American)

Practical Guidance: Persistence pays off and leads to success. Move toward the light.

Gort/Ivy Month Ceremony

Purpose

Honoring the Ivy portal. Celebrating our creativity and self-expression.

Preparation

Find pictures of the Milky Way or of DNA or of a labyrinth that leads into a center. Have folks bring their natal astrology charts with them if they have one. You will need a beautiful chalice or vase and a knife.

Prepare small cardboard squares that you can tie five or six strands of yarn or ribbon to from top to bottom—this will be for a weaving activity. If you cut into the tops and bottoms of the cardboard squares about a half inch, it is easy to set the strings. Cut various ribbons and yarn for each participant to use to weave into the strands on the squares that you have prepared.

Welcome and Greetings

Welcome to our Ivy month ceremony. Introduce yourself and go around the circle having each participant share their name and why they came to the circle. Have them close their eyes and share a moment of silence to prepare for the ceremony.

Call the Directions

Call in the directions and call in the plant spirit of Ivy (prophecy, the journey into the self) and her totems, guides, and deities (spider and wolf and the Goddesses of weaving.)

Teachings

This portal includes the energy of the sign of Leo and here we want to honor our will and purpose, our creativity, and our self-expression. Where do you want to shine in your life? In what area do you seek applause? Look at your natal chart and see in which house the sign of Leo falls. Also review which house your sun is in. Look at your fifth house as well. These are places where you want to be a star! Leo, the sun, and the fifth house are similar in their expressions. This is where you look to define your purpose, your path, and your reason to be. In this ritual we seek strengthening and empowerment as we align with our true purpose.

The symbol for our growth pattern is the spiral. (Show pictures you have of the spiral pattern.) Trace the pattern of a spiral into the center, and then out again. Close your eyes and see the pattern of a spiral; follow it into the center and out again. Imagine Ivy growing around a pole up toward the light.

This portal is represented by the Ivy that grows toward the light even when it is challenged to grow in the worst of environments. Ivy continues to grow toward the light as she spirals up and around in a continuous pattern. This is how we develop our lives. This is how we grow more refined lives and keep moving toward greater consciousness. Tonight, we define what we are moving and growing toward. We claim what we want to become!

Chant

> *What is the teaching of the Ivy? The light lives within.*
> *Our freedom comes from growing toward the light.*
> *Behold! We spiral toward our greater consciousness.*
> *And we are free to recreate ourselves at every moment.*
> *We seek guidance as we walk through our own inner*
> *labyrinth into the mystery*
> *What is the teaching of the Ivy? Persistence and peace.*

Activity

Pass a beautiful chalice or vase around the circle. Have each person place—energetically—what they are creating into the vase. Have them vocalize what they are placing into the caldron or chalice. Pass around a knife and have them use it to symbolically cut away any thoughts, feelings, or behaviors that block this creation. They can cut away what no longer serves them. Have them take a moment to really energize and visualize and honor what they have placed into that chalice. Then pass the experience on to the next person. When complete, read these words:

> We are all seeds of a new culture
> and a new world that is yet to come.

Let wisdom come to us.
We ask for guidance and courage as
we intentionally weave the best of our
resources, our aspirations, and our
creativity to make a new reality.
We ask for enlightenment as we learn
to trust and express our true nature.
We give gratitude.

Sing

Choose songs that have to do with the Goddess and with creativity.

Guided Meditation

Close your eyes and slow down your breath. Take some deep breaths. Allow yourself to become quiet and let go of your worries. Breathe and let yourself relax. Center yourself at your heart. There is a doorway here at the center of your heart. As you walk through the threshold, find yourself in a beautiful favorite place in nature. Take a moment to feel the safety of this place and know that you can return here anytime you so choose. Notice the terrain. The sun is warm and the sky blue and you are surrounded by this familiar place.

Imagine yourself in proximity to an ancient woman who is a master weaver. You see her from afar as she begins to walk toward you. She is a small woman and dressed in woven fabrics, with hints of nature added. You see feathers, shells, and gemstones added into her garment, her cloak, and her headdress. As she approaches you, she smiles, and you see the love she has for you in her bright eyes. This is the Goddess of weaving. In fact, it is she that weaves the fabric of our existence upon the material plane. She lives in the unseen realm, but she is willing to work with you today. She wears upon her body a cloak of weavings with many colors and many patterns. It is mesmerizing just to look at her.

As she looks at you she sees the patterns of your life. She sees the patterns of your habits and she sees your dysfunctions (don't worry, we all have this), and she sees this as part of your beauty. She looks at you with intense love and she accepts all. She also sees all your originality and color and magnificence. She asks you if she can have your permission to unweave a few strands here and there, do some reweaving, mending, and energizing. Nod if you are willing to have this master goddess attend to you.

She begins to work her magic. You hear her soft words and incantations. She unweaves patterns that you no longer need or that are causing your problems. She adjusts and reworks and frees up energy. Simply feel her at work, gently rebuilding and reweaving. She lets more light in and weaves in strands of love, joy, compassion, and freedom. Feel her love like honey and begin to see the beauty of you that she is working at ... (long pause)

When she is finished give her your gratitude and ask her to tell you what she did for you ... Take a moment to receive her information.

Now she gives you ribbon and a small hand loom, which already has the vertical strands in place. She asks you to begin to weave your ribbons into and through the ribbons that are already there. Go ahead and work your loom and place into it ribbons of love, abundance, fun, friendship, creativity, joy, flow, grace, ease, and any other positive words that come up for you. This is your symbol for reworking your life to include more of the joy of living. She tells you that just as you weave this piece of art, you also weave the art of your life. You do this through positive words, feelings, and actions. You do this through forgiveness and letting go. You do this through your gratitude. These are choices that you can make. When you are conscious of how you create, you can create a beautiful life. Take your time and enjoy the process of consciously working your own loom, your own life.

When your work with the Priestess of Weaving is complete, give your gratitude. Take a moment to think of the Ivy plant that is always moving toward the light. You too can choose light. Ground and center.

Sharing

Have your participants share their experiences.

Sing

Choose songs about spiraling into the center or weaving, or ones that honor the Goddess.

Chant

> We are weavers. We are woven.
> We are the warp and we are the weft.
> We are the magic creators. We weave
> the multicolored fabrics of our lives.
> The Goddess directs our hands with love.
> We create beauty everywhere we go.

Activity: Weaving Qualities into Our Lives

Pass out the small weaving cards and have each person weave in strands as they think about the qualities they want to build into their life.

Sharing

After enough time to work, allow them to share about what they wove into their piece and how they felt about the activity.

Ending

Give gratitude for the totems and guides of Ivy. (Sometimes spiders are attracted by the attention and will show up after a ceremony. Let the spiders know that as much as you honor them, you would like them to stay outside.) Release the directions and open the circle.

An Ivy Story: Spider

One of my first real memories as a toddler is of seeing a very large spiderweb. It was a beautiful early fall morning and I was outside; the web was above me on an overhanging trellis above our garage. As I looked up I saw this beautiful circular pattern full of dew drops and glistening in the new morning's sunshine. I was transfixed by this beauty. Ever since that experience I have been careful to catch and release spiders rather than kill them. To me, they create such beautiful pieces of art with every web they spin.

Spider as a totem first came to me in dream time. She was a great jumping Mexican tarantula with red and white spots on her back. In this dream she came down from the ceiling beams to my bed and met me at eye level. Again, there was the transfixing quality of our moment together. Although I was surprised by the spider, I also saw that she was beautiful, and I was awestruck. There was nothing scary about her. It seemed to me that we had a conversation without words and that it was about the use of personal power.

Ever since I learned Alchemical Healing, which is an energetic healing form that I now teach, spider has appeared as a totem to help me in my work. She can ethereally weave torn muscle or ligament and has been especially helpful in weaving gaskets over hernias or sewing hernias shut after she gently pushes the intestines back into their proper place. My husband tore the gasket that was sewn in by a surgeon to repair a hernia and we were very afraid that he would have to go back and have another surgery.

As we started our work together he began to have an inner vision that he reported to me. In his journey he saw spider show up and she asked him if she could do some repair work for him. He said yes. He then actually began to feel spider reweave the torn area. Afterward we gave our gratitude to spider, and he never has had another problem with his hernia.

A couple of years ago I did a ritual for Ivy. I invited spider to come as a guide as we called in the directions. We had a powerful and wonderful circle and I was happy with it. The next day, the hugest black spider I had ever seen walked across our living room floor. The next day another one showed up. And the next day another one came. My family and I were pretty sure we didn't want any more of these big black spiders in the house. I had to be the brave one and catch each one in a large glass and then release them into our yard with a blessing. I let the spirit of spider know that as much as I honored their weaving and appreciated all they do, I didn't want any more spiders to come visiting. I hoped we could continue our relationship with them outside. No more spiders showed up.

When you contemplate Ivy, you see her pattern of growth; she always moves toward the light and she is unstoppable. We grow in the same way as the Ivy. Sometimes when we are moving through our life we revisit an old wound. But remember, as we grow up and around our central selves, we are just visiting. We never relive what has gone before, but we see it from a different perspective.

You can always choose to create beauty. You can always choose to imbue the past with love, forgiveness, and the green persistent energy of Ivy. The best place to unite with the green energy is on the journey within. In this place there is a doorway to the mystery that offers you renewal, peace, and comfort. This is not a secret. Go there in silence and make space to listen and receive. This is the best vitamin of all time. In this quiet space you can connect with the light. This a passageway into greater consciousness.

After you have taken the journey to spend some time with your own inner life, bring that nourishment back out into the world. Think about what you are weaving or spinning. You are indeed a god or goddess and you are the master weaver of your own life. If you don't like something, you can take out a few strands of energy here and there and recreate the fabric of your existence with new choices. You can make an easy dance between the inner and the outer, the below and the above ... You can create the life you love that will enrich others as well. This is the teaching of Ivy.

ƝGETAL~ℝEED & GRASSES

September 5–October 2
Twelfth Lunation, September/October

Ogham: Ngetal (nyettle, ing-tal), Ng: ⁒

Keywords: Direct action, foster mothers, godmothers

Totems: Owl, pike

Deities: Cerridwen, the crone aspect of the Goddess

Practical Guidance: Set your intention. Take action. Every step you take gets you closer to your goals. Cut away what impedes. Go straight to the target.

Ngetal/Reed Month Ceremony

Holiday

The Fall Equinox is September 21/22.

Purpose

To honor the portal of the Reed month. Setting intentions. Taking steps toward fulfilling final dreams and aspirations for the end of the year.

Preparation

Collect grasses and display in a vase on the altar. If you have baskets place them on the altar to display the beauty and utilitarian uses of reeds and grasses.

Welcome and Greetings

Welcome to our Reed month ceremony. Introduce yourself and go around the circle having each participant share their name and why they came to the circle. Have them close their eyes and share a moment of silence to prepare for the ceremony.

Call the Directions

Call in the directions and invoke the energies of Reed (direct action) and the totems, guides, and deities (pike and owl). Call in the spirit of Reed. Call in the goddesses of the hunt, as well as the crone. Call in help for cutting through that which hinders and that which is ready to be recycled. Call in help for focus and aiming, as we choose what we want to manifest.

Teachings

The portal of Reed is a time when we begin to prepare for winter. This is a period when we gather up the last of the harvest. We gather and store the seeds. We cut away, recycle, and compost what is left from the harvest. We give our gratitude for the abundance of the passing season.

Reeds represent the stalks and grasses. The structures of these hollow reeds, bulrushes, bamboo, and papa grasses are hollow through the center, much like peashooters or flutes that require our breath to work. Likewise, we must breathe into our intentions to activate them. This is an important teaching of Reed. We are encouraged to become hollow so that spirit can work through us and increase our yield even beyond our imaginings. We can invite spirit to work through us by directing our intention—in effect becoming cocreators. And we must by necessity be willing to let go or cut away that which impedes us. We are reminded to let go of harmful, negative, and destructive habits that stand between our desires and our manifestation of those desires.

The Reeds protected Moses in the bulrushes until he was saved by his foster mother. The Reeds ask us to protect what is growing and vulnerable so that it can mature into its rightful heritage. This is the same for dreams, aspirations, projects, and ventures. Reed reminds us to protect our dreams and nurture them well until they are mature enough to be sent out into the world. Seek good foster parents. Find a godmother. These are people who can be trusted to speak for your greatest good and act as your protectors and encouragers. Seek good nurturers for your ventures.

Reed is a threshold month in which we can set and deliver our last intentions for the year's end. We acknowledge that what we have worked for requires only direction and intent to be brought into manifestation. When it is the right time, release your arrow toward your goal. This is the portal for that last thrust of intention. We give our gratitude for the summer's fertility and the bountiful harvest.

Read

> This portal is about the teachings of owl and pike. These are excellent models of hunting.
>
> They wait, and when the time is perfect they strike. They do not question. They act. In the same way, we will focus on a completion process for the year. What is the last great goal that you would like to see manifested in your life?

Sharing

Pass the talking stick and ask each person to think about what they will send their arrow of intention toward.

Chant

> *What is the teaching of the Reed?*
> *We create through our intentions.*
> *Our freedom comes through aiming*

our arrow and letting it fly.
Behold! We go straight for the last
aspiration of our year and let go.
Even as we protect our visions and
dreams until they are ready to be released.
We seek our crone's protection and guidance.
What is the teaching of the Reed? Spirit creates through us.

Sing

Sing and drum songs of your choosing, or simply allow songs and music to evolve, knowing that the energy of the circle will appear and make itself known.

Guided Meditation

Close your eyes and slow your breath. Bring your attention to your heart and feed it with love. Allow yourself to slow down and to breathe deeply as we begin to journey together. Breathe in this way for a few moments as you adjust to the peace that is offered to you here in this inner place.

You find yourself traveling to a lovely forest. It is a fall day and you find yourself walking under an umbrella of trees just at dusk. You can smell the heavenly scent of the cedars and firs. Dappled sun filters through and creates a lovely pattern upon the path before you. All around you is a colorful carpet of fallen leaves. They rustle as you move along. You see golden, red, and yellow leaves gently falling from the tree branches above you, although many still cling to their branches, waiting for a stronger wind to release them.

You notice the call of an owl and you stop to find her. You see her up in the branch on the tree just before you. Even though it is growing a bit darker you feel no fear. You know that this forest is a place of safety for you and that the owl wants to communicate with you.

You can see the bright yellow eyes of your snowy owl and she flies on down to sit upon your shoulder. You feel the wind of her motion as she sweeps down to you. She makes soft sounds and nibbles gently upon

your ear. Owl is a great hunter even in the dark, since she is noctur-
nal. She knows how to direct her energy toward her target. She doesn't
think about the "what ifs"; she goes for what she sees. She has much to
teach about direct action. Take a moment to listen to her message…

Owl is also the symbol for wisdom. What wisdom does owl have for
you today? (Pause) What questions do you have for owl? What do you
want to happen in your life? What are your goals, your aspirations, or
your big dreams? Allow owl to show you a blueprint for action. Let her
show you the steps. Is there anything standing in the way? What do you
need to let go of? Are you willing to make some changes that will ensure that your dreams can become reality? Are you willing to take some
action to move closer to your goals? If yes, tell owl that you are committed, and she will be glad to stay close as an ally.

It is time to leave the forest and your new ally. Remember that she is
as close as your call. Give your gratitude and bring yourself home from
the journey. Return slowly and when you are ready, open your eyes.
Ground and center.

Sharing

Pass the stick and let each person tell about their experience. What is
their goal? What steps will they begin to move toward their goal? Ask
them to remember the power of owl as their ally.

Activity: Choosing Your Own Fairy Godmother

Ask each participant to choose a real-life person that could act as their
fairy godmother. This should be a person that is encouraging and positive and whom they can share their goal or dream with. Have them
strategize with their helper. Have them think of this person as their
own personal lifeguard, cheerleader, and coach to help move their
dream out into the world. Encourage them to connect with this person
in the next week. (At the next circle or in the weeks to come, make sure
you get feedback from your circle members about their goals and how
they did.)

Finally, have each participant close their eyes and imagine a target set up with a bull's-eye a good distance away from them. Their goal becomes that target. Have them take a moment to focus on that goal.

Read

> See the target as your goal. Take an arrow from the quiver upon your back and set it into your sturdy bow. With a deep breath, pull back your bow with strength and knowing, and when ready, release an arrow that flies exactly to the center. Take a moment to feel the joy of having hit the mark. See your goal as already met. See your success. Really feel that … and know that what you want is already yours.

Ending

Close with healing prayers for friends and relatives and give gratitude for this harvest time of year. Open the circle by releasing the directions, the totems, the gods and goddesses, and the spirit at the center of all that is.

A Reed Story: Letting Go

In September of 1999, I attended a four day retreat out on the Pacific Ocean at La Push, Washington. I was aware that September is Reed's month and I purposefully gathered reeds and grasses as I walked the land to collect materials to make a shield. As we made our "medicine shields" in a process of silence, I pondered on the power of the grasses, pampas, reeds, cattails, and other long-stemmed, hollow plants.

In circle I shared about the intent of becoming a hollowed reed for spirit to enter and work through me. We talked about letting go of what hinders. We talked about the use of the arrow to aim and let go toward our final desire of the year. For me that was the success of my workshops, classes, and ceremonies planned for October and my desire to make enough money to add to my husband's salary, so we could move through October in a good way, financially.

It was great to watch the impact of these teachings on the women in my circle. Everyone responded to the idea of aim and accuracy. One woman had brought owl feathers and placed eight of them on her shield. One woman put beautiful long grasses on her shield to represent making herself available for spirit to work through her. All of us responded to the idea that it takes effort to get the movement going, whether we use a straw for sucking, play a flute with the focus of our breath, or blow a pea through a shooter toward its destination. Think of the power and accuracy of a hunter in the Amazon with his blow dart. And certainly, hitting our target with accuracy takes focus and intention. All of us responded to the idea of getting that one last project or intention set and completed before the fall composting and the darkness of winter. And the idea of letting go of what no longer serves was something we all took into consideration.

Out on the beach I picked up stones to represent what I was now ready to bury and let go of. I asked Mother Earth to receive the energy and transmute it to its higher purpose. I released the three circles or groups that I had just recently ended, blessing each for its teachings. I also released the relationship with my daughter that represented her little girl self. Although she will always be my little girl, I was now prepared to relate to her as the young woman that she had become. This would take intelligence, flexibility, and willingness to change on my part. And finally, I released the relationship as I have known it with my son. He was ready to leave the nest, and I was ready to push if I must. I buried what we had created so far with love—to make room for the new. He was responsible for his own life and I needed to let go.

Contemplating these guides and totems, honoring the last harvestings, and noticing the power of this time of year as a portal for completion was a great encouragement for me. The other women seemed grateful for the information and used it readily in the creation process of their shield. I often wondered if anyone really cared about the teachings the Celtic tree calendar that so eloquently moves us through the seasonal changes. I was shown just how powerful these teachings from spirit can be. In the end my friend gifted me with a wonderful owl feather which, to me, represented wisdom.

It was easy to do my work out there as I felt supported by the Native ancestors of the land. Spirit was talking continuously through the ocean, the sky, the weather, the birds, and the whales. I found a most perfect pelican feather. When I came home, I looked up the astrological Sabian symbol to the degree of my moon in Dane Rudhyar's *An Astrological Mandala*, which I remembered had to do with pelicans. It said this: "Pelicans menaced by the behavior and refuse of men seek safer areas for bringing up their young."

Rudhyar goes on to explain, "Our technological society is polluting not only the global environment, but the minds and feeling responses of new generations as well. The search for a new way of life is seen by many people to be imperative."

Pelican is a good teacher for parents. Because my letting go had to do with my children and had to do with making outward and inner changes that provided good parenting for them, I was grateful. I also thought that these teachings had much to offer in giving me the courage I need to stay strong. The life that I desire for the next seven generations is supported by the many indigenous cultures around the world that teach reverence and connection to the natural world and the spirit realm. I am grateful to the Quileute tribe for protecting the land that I was able to do my spirit quest on, and I am grateful for the reminder to stay close to nature and to protect Gaia. Doing ceremony, following nature, and allowing for spirit work in retreat are ways I can keep the circle of renewal and regeneration going. I am encouraged to keep on with my work with the Celtic tree calendar and to continue with my teaching and writing.

As you contemplate the teachings of Reed, consider this: What in your life requires focus and direction? What goal or dream or desire requires the effort of intention so that it might grow its wings and fly? What must you let go of that might be standing in your way? What is ending? Can you create a ceremony to honor what is completed? What is begging for new life? What is spirit trying to create through you if you will only say yes?

STRAIF–BLACKTHORN
September 5–October 2
Shares the month with Ngetal/Reed

Ogham: Straif, Ss, St, Z:

Keywords: Negativity, negation, cleansing, perception, protection

Totems: Birds associated with death, such as the vulture

Guides and Deities: The Crone Goddesses, the Grim Reaper, dark, death, and underworld gods and goddesses

Practical Guidance: This too shall pass.

Straif/Blackthorn Month Ceremony
Purpose
Accepting negativity as a teacher.

Preparation
Find a branch with thorns for display on the altar or choose a picture or make a drawing of thorns. Perhaps place a rose with thorns in a vase for the altar.

Welcome and Greetings

Welcome to our Blackthorn month ceremony. Introduce yourself and go around the circle having each participant share their name and why they came to the circle. Have them close their eyes and share a moment of silence to prepare for the ceremony.

Call the Directions

Call in the directions and invoke the energies of Blackthorn (negation, negativity, cleansing, perception) and the totems, guides, and deities (Crone Goddesses, the Grim Reaper). Invoke the energy of the Blackthorn and give gratitude for its protection and its powers. We honor negativity as it is our master teacher and we embrace its purpose, accepting its presence and lessons.

Teachings

The main lesson from Blackthorn is to accept the negativity that comes into your life and to breathe through the experiences knowing that they will pass as all storms do. Part of what causes great suffering is the resistance we have to what we call negativity or failure. Blackthorn encourages us to move to a position of neutrality and to view our situation from a higher perspective. This tree offers protection as we pass through a difficult period. She asks us to stay positive and learn from the situation. What are the lessons?

Activity: Having Fun Releasing Negativity

Today we acknowledge and invite into the circle our negative thoughts, feelings, and situations with a bitching session. Pass a talking stick and take turns "bitching" to release negative emotions. Have your participants direct the energy into the bowl placed within the center of your circle. For instance, "I hate Republicans. I hate Democrats. I hate neo-Nazis. I hate doing dishes. I hate people who are stupid..."

Enjoy the display of negativity within this sacred space. It can be fun, funny, and quite cathartic.

When the group feels complete, symbolically burn the energetic negativity assembled in an earthen bowl. Say: "Know in your bones that you are free. You have emptied your story. You have created a new slate. Blessed be and so it is!"

Chant

> What is the teaching of the Blackthorn? Difficulty is our teacher.
> Our freedom comes from moving through our struggles.
> Behold! We transform within our troubles and rise to new perspectives.
> And we are free to learn from our challenges.
> We seek to open to greater truth.
> What is the teaching of the Blackthorn? This too shall pass.

Activity: Cleaning Our Slates

Have the group close their eyes and imagine they are holding their slate, which is full of writings about failures and disappointments and negative situations. Then have them clean their slate with a special cloth.

Then, upon their clean slate, in their mind's eye, have them each write a lesson they have learned from a difficult situation or event. Most people can see lessons learned and new possibilities that showed up for them after the chaos ended. This is one of the major teachings of this tree.

Sharing

Have them share how they felt when they cleared their slates. What lessons have they learned from a difficult situation? What new possibilities showed up?

Read

> It is our fierce attachment and identification to our bodies and our ego perceptions of separation that must be reevaluated. From the spiritual perspective, there is no judgment about events as positive or negative; they just are. And they

can be used for the evolution of greater compassion, understanding, and consciousness. They can be helpful to motivate us toward the actualization of love if we set that as our
higher purpose through all things.

Send love to all the dark places on the planet. Send love
to the hearts of people who choose to feed the negativity in
their life and who refuse to transform this energy and use it
for their own transformation. Send love to that which is inside all of us that holds fear, hatred, and judgment.

(Take a moment of silence together to do this.)

Sing

Choose a song that connects your group to spirit. Choose songs of acceptance, forgiveness, and starting over.

Chant

> Move from your fear to your love.
> Move from your hate to your forgiveness.
> Let the old story go.
> Begin again.
> Create a story of love.

Guided Meditation

Imagine yourself in a grove of Blackthorn trees. They are thick and
strong, and you notice their menacing thorns. You might think about
sayings like "He's a thorn in my side" or "This is a thorny situation."
Jesus wore a crown of thorns. Take a moment to examine your own
feelings about thorns.

It is true that thorns suggest negativity and difficulty. They also can
be very protective. They can keep out that which is dangerous. They
act as a border or fence. What do you need to protect in your life right
now? Ask the trees to help protect you and help you to hold that which

is most important and most joyful and most sacred in your life. Ask them to remind you to protect these things.

Think of something that is troubling you right now and lay it right at the trunk of one of the Blackthorn trees. Look at your trouble as you lay it on the ground. Does it look different to you from this new perspective? Ask Blackthorn how you might best navigate this situation. Does the grove have encouragement for you that this too shall pass? You will notice an infusion of courage and knowing. Give your gratitude to the grove. If you pick up your trouble it may seem lighter and you may notice a silver lining in the cloud above, or you might choose to leave the energy with the trees altogether. They will transmute the negativity and return it to Mother Earth, who will know how to best use it.

It is time to gently come back to the ceremony and ground and center. When you are ready, you may open your eyes.

Sharing

Have your participants share their experiences.

Sing

Choose ending songs or songs that call upon spirit for guidance and healing.

Ending

Give gratitude to the teachings of the Blackthorn tree and all the helpers. Open the circle by thanking and releasing the four directions and the center. Thank the gods and goddesses that were evoked and all the totems and spirit helpers. Especially thank the Blackthorn for its healing properties and energies that have blessed us this month.

A Blackthorn Story: Lessons from the Grim Reaper

The most "negative story" I can think of was the day my mother died of an accidental drowning. I must tell you that a month or so before her death we had resolved some difficult issues between us and she had asked me to forgive her. That meant a lot to me. I also have to say that she had spent some time looking at one of my paintings and asking me why I put the Grim Reaper in such a beautiful piece of art. My answer was that death was a part of life, and the Reaper was a guide to navigate the entrance to a new life of experience—which is how I saw death. He just had to be in the painting; he showed up, so to speak. Little did I know that the Grim Reaper would soon be tapping my mother on her shoulder.

My mother drowned on July 28, 1985. On the day that my mother died I kept hearing the phone ring, but every time I went to the phone it was not actually ringing. I even heard it when I was outside unleashing the dog and ran back into the house, only to see that the phone was silent.

The next time I heard the phone ring I could see that the phone in front of me was truly not ringing. I decided to pick up the ringing phone in my mind and through my imagination. I closed my eyes and gave myself over to the experience. The call was from my sister-in-law, Willa, and she asked me to sit down, which I promptly did. She proceeded to tell me that my mother had accidentally drowned. She told me that Mom had died while swimming in shallow water at a party on Hoods Canal.

With these words in my head, I abruptly ended the conversation. Why would I choose to have such morbid thoughts on such a beautiful Seattle summer day? I thought I must be truly crazy, so I went on with my chores of feeding the dog, getting the dinner out of the freezer, and sorting the clothes for the next load of laundry. I got some Play-Doh out for my three-year-old son and he began to make some pretend hamburgers, which he tried to feed to the dog.

About an hour or so later, the phone did ring. When I picked it up it was the voice of my sister-in-law, Willa, and I knew what she was going to say when she told me to sit down. Indeed, my mother had drowned, and I was stunned.

The next few days I felt as if I was wrapped in a batting of shock and grief. I went and met with my other siblings at my father's rented home on the Olympic Peninsula. There were a multitude of arrangements to be made and a lot of tears were shared. We all coped by doing a lot of cooking and baking for the upcoming memorial service. Our emotions seemed to come in waves that carried my family into bouts of crying and hugs. We all stayed together until after the funeral and I did not choose to tell anyone about the phone experiences.

After the funeral I returned home to Seattle. I expected to feel sad and upset, but I did not expect what came next. That night as I attempted to go to sleep, I felt my mother's presence. The room became terribly cold and I was so frightened that I couldn't move or make a sound. I was terrified. I couldn't see my mother, but I did feel her presence and she was hysterical. She was absolutely panicked, and she demanded that I help her.

It was upsetting, to say the least, that what seemed to be happening to my mother was not a peaceful passing. I had hoped for rest for my mom and an end to her unhappiness and lack of fulfillment in the later part of her life. I had hoped for a release into a better world or realm. My mom's drinking in the last few years had worried me, and I knew mom was in trouble. I had hoped that her death would be a positive release or going home.

Again, I was plagued with a sense that I must be making this up and that I was the victim of an overactive imagination driven by grief. I thought I was having this experience because of the stress over this sudden death and accident. I chastised myself for playing mind games, especially because it seemed a rather cruel thing to create in light of the loss of my mother.

But then I reminded myself of that phone call in my head. I had forgotten that in all the activity and funeral proceedings. That had been real. And what I was experiencing now felt real. My mother's energy field, if I can call it that, was not visible, and yet it was palpable. She seemed to be attacking me. She came from above me and grabbed my throat and shoulders as if to wake me up. I felt her weight and her force upon my chest. She wanted me to see her, and she wanted whatever was happening to her to stop. She wanted me to fix it and make it all go away.

My mother didn't seem to have a clue that she had died. She wanted me to relieve her intense fear. She was desperate and violent with me. I could hardly breathe. I felt all the air being sucked out of me. And I couldn't move to yell for help or to get out of my bed. I spent the whole night like that. Feeling her weight and desperate communications, hearing my own criticism for creating the experience, and not being able to reach out even to my husband, who slept next to me, I lay there freezing and yet sweating in fear. Finally, the energy subsided with the rising of the sun. I had been awake all night, too terrified to move or speak, and I felt like I had been gripped by death itself.

I was exhausted and confused. I really did not want this contact, nor did I know how to proceed. I didn't want the same thing to happen when I went to sleep again. I wanted to grieve in peace, and I felt angry. My mom had already extracted enough "mothering" from me throughout our relationship and now it felt that she was sucking the life out of me from her grave. Why couldn't she just move on like all the other dead people? Why was she stuck and why was she coming to me? This all felt so unfair. Here I was in shock and grief and if I told anybody else what had happened I knew they'd think I was loony. And with everyone else in the family so upset, it would be too cruel to bring this up. And who do you go to with problems like this…? And so I decided I didn't have to be a party to this interaction. I wasn't sure why this was happening to me and not to someone else. Perhaps I did possess a certain sensitivity or openness or clairvoyance, but I was going to say a big "NO" to working with dead people in general, especially relatives and especially my mother.

So, I sat down and got very quiet. I began to repeat within, "Go toward the light, Mom, go toward the light. I can't help you. I can't save you. This is your death and you must travel it by yourself. You can't get out of it, and you indeed have died. You drowned. I do not want you here, and you cannot get anything from me. I can do nothing to help you. I am closing the door. You need to move on toward the light now." With those words the atmosphere around me seemed to change. My mother did not visit me again and I placed this experience quietly to bed within myself and did not speak of it again.

One day some five years later I was listening to my husband tell me about the experiences he had when his mother died of cancer. He described being at his mom's bedside when she died. His mom, Nancy, had a peaceful passing, and it was a very moving and touching story. After he told me the story, I blurted out with strong emotion, "You are so lucky. Your mom didn't accost you, scare the living daylights out of you, and even try to get you to change places with her like my mom did." I was surprised by the power of my outburst and I realized that I was still very angry at my mom. Yet somehow, I felt sheepish for my remarks. Somehow I felt that I was hurting my mom's memory with my words.

The next day I mistakenly threw my favorite earrings in the washing machine when I was washing a pile of clothes they had carelessly been placed on. Those earrings had belonged to my mom. They were bought in Bali and they were elongated silver baubles that were hand-painted in turquoise with dots of red and pink. When I discovered them in the bottom of the machine, all the color had washed out of them. I felt heartsick and associated the loss with those harsh words about my mother. The strange thing was that I felt I had a right to be angry, but I also had a strong intuition that my mom didn't feel that she deserved this anger. I sensed that Mom was communicating with me and was not happy about that remark I had made. I sensed that mom thought it was time for me to take another look at that experience and perhaps consider forgiveness.

A week later I happened to turn to a TV show about people's experiences with visits from dead loved ones. Almost all the stories were quite beautiful and healing. I remembered thinking, "Well, I bet no one is going to tell a story like mine." But indeed, there was a young woman who reported a visitation from a boyfriend who had died, and she physically felt him grab her and try to forcefully take her with him. She said she was terrified. The expert asked the woman if he had died suddenly and unexpectedly. She said yes. The expert explained that this occurs because the loved one doesn't understand that they are dead, and they panic when no one sees them or will communicate with them. They often will approach a "sensitive" member of the family, whom they try desperately to contact.

"Oh," I thought. "Maybe my mom wasn't such a bad lady after all. Maybe she was just doing what people do when they die without warning. They are shocked and scared and trying to get back to life as usual, but no one even sees them. They have no intention of passing over gracefully, because they don't even know that they are dead! And they don't understand the fear they are causing."

I now could better understand the feelings I had over my outburst, and those earrings had really captured my attention even though I hated to lose them. I decided to have a little chat with my mom. I wanted to say that I was sorry and that I hadn't understood. I wondered why it was so damn difficult to get important information in this culture. The information regarding the afterlife and the process of crossing over was not in the encyclopedia. I am grateful that times have changed and that there is much more information available and there is less fear and skepticism about such topics.

I sat down and closed my eyes and had a dialogue with Mom, which I thoroughly enjoyed. It was an internal dialogue, but it felt real. I felt that my mom had passed over and was happy and peaceful now. I also appreciated that my mom could send messages to me through dreams and coincidences and synchronicities. I also appreciated that she didn't have to get too physical anymore to get my attention. I still miss those earrings. But when I see them tucked safely in my jewelry box, all stripped down to their original silver, I just laugh. So, no more hard feelings and no more bad-mouthing my mom.

I have to say that as difficult as that experience was in the moment and as terrified as I was, there was an internal knowing that got me through, and in time I did get the information I needed to understand what happened. It has been my experience that things have happened to me before I had any understanding. Those experiences propelled me to study outside of the cultural consensus reality that I lived in. I was able to enlarge my view about the true nature of reality. I do not regret the experiences, even though at times I was ill-equipped to understand them.

One of my hopes when describing many of these experiences is that my readers will have a more normalized understanding of their own experiences that don't fit into ordinary everyday Western culture reality. So, in viewing the meaning of Straif, I can look at "strife" in a different context. I can accept that meaning will come after the difficulty if I can just hang in there with my own knowing, faith, and trust. I have always come to intense learning and study after these experiences and the meaning of them always brings renewal and regeneration to my life.

How do we overcome adversity when it comes to us? The teaching of Blackthorn is that it will pass. There is protection for you. During any difficult period or challenge, the best teaching from the trees is the cyclical nature of our reality. Like any weather, storms always pass. The sun comes out again. The light will return.

When you contemplate the teaching of the Blackthorn and you review your own dark nights of the soul, what do you learn? How is your character strengthened? What do you learn about yourself? What do you glean about your own strength and resolve? Were the trials meaningful in any way as your teachers? Were they purposeful?

All the most painful periods of my life have been my best teachers. Divorce taught me what was most important to me in life. Dealing with toxic mold and my hypersensitivity to chemicals forced me to change my thinking about everything. A bout with Cipro antibiotic toxicity brought me to my knees, but I healed, and I knew that if I kept my mind clear and strong, it would pass. And I know that when the angel comes for me, my death will not be an end to my consciousness. I move from fear to love. I move from rage to compassion.

Death, pain, disease, loss—all have their lessons and teachings. How we go through our difficult times marks our character. The task is to continue to move from fear to love and from resistance to acceptance. I am not saying that the process of grief is an easy one. Working through challenges may take every fiber of your being and I support you, the reader, in your own process. And yet I also suggest looking at the situation from a higher perspective. Allow the negativity to be your teacher. This is the teaching of Blackthorn.

Fall Equinox Ceremony
September 21/22

The autumnal equinox celebrates equal day and night, and the preparation of winter. This is the time of the final harvest and is an early
Thanksgiving celebration. Fall has arrived and we say goodbye to the
sun as we prepare for winter. Another name is Mabon.

Purpose

To celebrate the equinox.

Preparation

Make small squares of paper to write down what participants are ready
to let go of. Prepare a large bowl with earth and a central candles in-
which participants can burn their squares of paper.

Welcome and Greetings

Welcome to our Fall Equinox ceremony. Introduce yourself and go
around the circle having each participant share their name and why
they came to the circle. Have them close their eyes and share a moment
of silence to prepare for the ceremony.

Call the Directions

Call in the directions and the energies of the autumnal equinox.

Teachings

Tonight, we come together to celebrate a time of equal day and night
as we move toward the darkest night of the year and winter. We bid the
light of the god Lugh and the goddess Lucina (Nordic) farewell. We say
goodbye to our diminishing days of sunshine. This is the time of the
final harvest and gratitude is an important part of this early Thanksgiving celebration. We gather the last of the harvest and we store the

seeds and food for winter. We gather the fruits and vegetables from the gardens. The leaves fall from the trees with the increasing winds and changes in the weather. Now is the time to gather your herbs, seeds, and leaves to add to your medicine supplies.

Another name for this holiday is Mabon. Mabon is a time of repose and rest after the labors of the harvest. We compost, mulch, recycle, and clear our gardens for winter. This is a time to turn inward and let go of that which has not borne fruit in our personal lives. Demeter (Greek) lets go of her dear daughter Persephone as she descends to the underworld. What do you have to let go of that is near and dear to you? Herne the Hunter hunts down the stag and becomes the great horned god Cernunnos. The stag/god gives up its life for the people; the vegetation god sacrifices the fruit and seeds of his labor; corn and wheat are ground into flour. Soon the stag will die and his crown of antlers will return to the earth. Soon the vegetation will be reaped and what remains can be composted back into the earth to feed her with nutrients.

We honor that which dies so that we may live. We honor the fruits of the trees, the vegetables of the garden, the wheat and grains and vines, the animals, and all that sustains us. We honor all of life. We honor the elements that sustain us, and we give blessing to our Mother Earth, Gaia. We honor the crone aspect of the Great Mother. She is the Grim Reaper, *and* she is the midwife. She allows that which has died to replenish the earth so that all may grow again. She is the end and the beginning.

Sing

Choose songs that have to do with autumn, or the crone aspect of the Goddess.

Chant

> *What is the teaching of the Fall Equinox? Regeneration.*
> *Our freedom comes from releasing our past as we bid adieu to the sun.*
> *Behold! The crone returns to reap what we have sown.*
> *And we are free to let go of that which has not borne fruit.*

We seek to give our gratitude for another cycle of life.
What is the teaching of the Fall Equinox? Go within and rest.

Read

We recognize this time of year as a time of being rather than of doing. We celebrate caves and quiet spaces. We let go of striving. We honor shadows and interior places. We go within. This is where all regeneration takes places. Although we do strive to fulfill our ambitions, this is a time to rest after the work of cleaning things away. We honor what is now barren, in preparation for what will grow. We clean our gardens and pull out the weeds and that which is left over after the harvesting; that which is done. We watch as the bear readies herself for hibernation, the birds begin to fly south, and the squirrels are busy foraging. We watch the leaves turn colors and fall to the ground. We take care of the residue.

We recycle and compost the leaves that are left. Take a moment to think about what you are done with. Are you willing to let go of it all like the tree must let go of its leaves? Are you ready for another turn around the wheel? Are you prepared to enter the dark?

Sing

Choose songs that celebrate fall and honor the trees, the mystery, and the ancestors.

Chant

The wheel turns again.
We welcome you, the portal of equal day and night.
We welcome our crone on this autumn day.
She is the end and the beginning.
She is our mystery.

Activity: Letting Go

Pass out a small square of paper and a pencil or pen to each person. Have them make a list of that which they are done with. Then have them fold their papers into triangles and let each person feed their paper to the flame with their blessings. Allow that energy to return to the void so that it can be used again to create something new. As each participant goes to the flame they say: "I bless that which I let go of. I feed it to the fire of creativity. I know that the ashes of my creation will feed the creation of something new."

Go around the circle and have each participant say: "I give this time to laying fallow the garden and resting. And to speak of that which I am grateful for."

Have each one share what they are grateful for as they count their blessings.

Read

> Now we begin our movement toward the dark half of the year. We begin reaching toward the darkness. Do not be afraid of the dark. Let's use this little bit of precious time to honor just being, to unconditionally accept ourselves.

Guided Meditation

Take these few moments of meditation to simply be with yourselves and to breathe deeply. (Play some sweet music, turn off the lights, and allow the group to breathe together in silent meditation.)

Sharing

Have the participants share their experiences in the meditation.

Sing

Choose ending songs or songs that express the mystery.

Endings

Open the circle by thanking and releasing the four directions and the center. Thank the gods and goddesses that were evoked and all the totems and spirit helpers.

RUIS–ELDER

October 3–October 30
Thirteenth Lunation, October

Ogham: Ruis (roush, roo-ish), R:

Keywords: Elders, grandmothers and clan keepers, renewal, death and rebirth, transformation, the passing of the soul from the physical realm to the spiritual, the crane bag (wisdom)

Totems: Cranes, storks, and the ibis

Guides and Deities: The crone aspect of the Goddess:

- Scotland—Cailleach, Carline, Mag-Moullach, or Bera
- Britain—the old hag, the Sowain Goddess
- Wales—Cerridwen
- Ireland—Sheela-na-gig
- Death and underworld goddesses, ancestors

Practical Guidance: Healing and transformation are yours.

Ruis/Elder Month Ceremony

Purpose

Celebrating the Elder portal. Reviewing the year and giving gratitude to the elders, ancestors, those who have passed through the veil, and our guides, totems, and helpers. Letting go.

Preparation

Ask participants to bring their journal. Collect or sew one small bag for each of your participants, to be introduced as crane bags. Cranes were the repository of the mystical moon wisdom of the Celts, and their bags held charms, incantations, poetry, stories and myths, songs, scripts and symbols—the collective wisdom of the Druids. These can be a sack or silk purse or any kind of little bag that will be used to hold good medicine and magic tools. Prepare affirmations on strips of folded paper. Prepare small squares of paper to be burned. Provide pens or pencils. Fan a tarot deck out facedown on the altar.

Welcome and Greetings

Welcome to our Elder month ceremony. Introduce yourself and go around the circle having each participant share their name and why they came to the circle. Have them close their eyes and share a moment of silence to prepare for the ceremony.

Call the Directions

Call the directions and invoke the energies of Elder (transformation, death and rebirth, endings) and the totems, guides, and deities (crane, stork, ibis, crone aspects of the Goddess). At the center call the Winged Ones. Call the goddesses Maat (Egyptian) and Hecate (Greek) and the mother vulture goddess Mut (Egyptian). Call in the crones of the British Isles.

Teachings

Elder is a threshold month and a corridor because it marks the last month of the year and the end of the growing season. This was a time to save the seeds and prepare for the winter. Because there was no guarantee that the people would make it through the long, cold, barren months, this was a period to think about death, and let go of grudges and resentments. This was a time to understand that death is a doorway we all walk through so that we may join our loved ones on the other side who are waiting for us with love. Other themes that fall under the Elder tree's governance are completions and endings, looking over the year and deciding what no longer serves or was created but is limiting, and honoring our ancestors and lineages.

This is a wisdom portal and the totem helpers are the Winged Ones, especially the ibis, stork, and crane. These birds are wisdom carriers with the ability to fly between the worlds and retrieve information. This is a time to seek guidance from those who have passed over. This is a time when we can remember our loved ones and our ancestors. The crone is especially revered. This is a time of deep gratitude for all that has gone before us and all that will come after. As we take stock of the year, it is a time to let go. It is also a time for forgiveness and healing.

Chant

> What is the teaching of the Elder? Transformation.
> Our freedom comes from accepting death as new life.
> Behold! We die in our endings and are rebirthed
> in our new beginnings.
> And we are free to become our true nature.
> We seek the wisdom of our elders and our ancestors.
> What is the teaching of the Elder? Forgive. Let go.

Sing

Choose songs that honor the three aspects of the Goddess and especially the crone, as well songs that have to do with transformation and the Winged Ones.

Activity: Maat (Egypt) and Reviewing the Year

Show your group a picture of Maat. You can print one out easily enough from the internet. Maat is an Egyptian goddess of wisdom and inner truth and she wears an ostrich feather upon her headdress. She protects each soul through the journey of spiritual evolution. She is ancient wisdom that urges us toward truth. She urges you to look at the balance and imbalance in your life. Maat is also the goddess of justice, judgment, equanimity, and fairness. She holds the world in balance and creates order out of confusion.

Have each person take a moment to meet with Maat in their mind's eye and to envision her. Have them ask Maat to help them review the past year that began last November 1. They can write their review in their journals. Take a good bit of time with this.

Have each person consider what they choose to compost and recycle from the year. These can be attitudes and beliefs, emotions, circumstances, relationships, behaviors, or old patterns. Have them ask the vulture goddess mother Mut/Nekhbet (Egypt) or falcon to help them pick and choose that which is ready to go. She does this with her sharp beak and her keen eyesight. Have them write these down on a piece of paper.

Pass a dish so that each participant can burn their paper. A large abalone shell works well for this, or an earthenware bowl with dirt in it. Keep the paper small. They can talk about what they are letting go, or they can choose silence.

After each person burns their paper, everyone repeats:

All that is burned here is released.
We ask the Crone Goddesses to
help in this composting process.

What we let go of becomes energy for what
we will create, and we ask the crone's blessings.

Guided Meditation

(Turn off the lights and light one candle at the center of your altar.) Close your eyes and begin to pay attention to your breath. Slow it down a bit. Notice where you are holding any tension in your body. Allow that to go. Relax and breathe. Place your attention on your heart and feed your heart with love. Allow that love to fill every cell of your body. Relax into that love. Take a few more very deep breaths as you enter the silence ... (pause)

Tonight, we wish also to honor our ancestors, and thank them for all their gifts. Take a moment to consider this ...

Return to the lands from which you hail. Pick the country that you feel the most affinity with. Travel within until you come to just the right place ... (pause)

Here you are greeted by people who seem to know you already. You find yourself meeting your relatives and ancestors. There is no sense of fear here. You experience a sense of delight to have the opportunity to meet these people. They are openhearted with you and they let you know that you are part of the family. In the background you hear singing and music and you know it represents the country that you have chosen. It feels right to be able to be here in this place, on this ground, and with these people.

Here you see that the elders have a special place of honor. These people of age are wise and they are respected. An old wise woman comes to you and takes your hand. You notice just how ancient this crone is when you feel and see her hands. Yet when you look into her eyes she has great joy and merriment to share with you. You feel her deep unconditional love. She has words of wisdom to share with you about your life. Take some time with her to absorb her messages ...

When you feel complete, give your gratitude to your wise one, and to the rest of your clan. Give gratitude to your homeland and know that you can return anytime you want. These people know all about you and they are in your corner always wanting the very best for you. Give them kisses and hugs and handshakes as you say goodbye. Return to this time and space, ground and center, and when you are ready, open your eyes.

Sharing

Have your group share their experiences with the group.

Activity: Working with the Ancestors

Have your circle think of the blessings from ancestors, relatives, and friends that have passed on to the otherworld. Have them consider what they no longer desire to carry for these people. Perhaps there is a legacy, a promise, an addiction, an attitude that you wish to return to its proper owner. Pass the stick and have the circle share what they will carry on and what they will no longer carry.

Sing

Choose songs that honor the ancestors. Now, consider the world of the spirit helpers and totems. Choose songs expressing gratitude, especially to the Winged Ones who help navigate between the worlds.

Activity: Giving Gratitude, Divination, and the Crane Bag Affirmation

Pass a feather and have your participants speak gratitude for what they are blessed with, as we migrate into the new year.

Have each participant choose a tarot card from a deck fanned out on the altar for the new year. Each participant can share what the card means to them.

Pass out crane bags and talk about the meaning. The crane bag was extra special wisdom teaching said to have been a gift from the sea god Manannan. It held the forfeda (the last five ogham of the alphabet), which held the collective wisdom of the ancient cosmology. These personal bags can hold feathers, stones, crystals and gemstones, rocks, charms, incantations, ogham, runes, affirmations, and other meaningful messages or objects of magic.

Have them pick an affirmation from the bowl that you have set on the altar. This is full of affirmations written on strips of paper that you have prepared ahead of time. Have them read their affirmation out loud so that the group can witness it. They can take their wisdom bag and their affirmation home to place upon their own altar.

Ending

Thank the gods and goddesses that were evoked and all the totems and spirit helpers. Especially thank the Elder tree for its healing properties and energies that have blessed us this month. Open the circle by thanking and releasing the four directions and the center.

An Elder Story: The Ancestors Have Something to Say

I was at the first class of Nicki Scully's Alchemical Healing series, which was held at Starfeather's lodge in Edmonds, Washington, and a wonderful woman named Kathryn Ravenwood was leading us on a guided journey to commune with our ancestors. A guided meditation is a wonderful way to contact your ancestors. We were working with forgiveness. In my mind's eye, I traveled with bees that took me to two beautiful gardens. One was in central England. There I met with my English lineage through my mother's side of the family. The other was in Swansea, Wales, which is the home of my father's Welsh lineage.

In the lovely English garden, I spoke with my maternal great-great-great-grandfather, who had been a merchant. I recognized him from old family photos. He came right up to me with a mission on his mind. He told me that he was sorry—for he had very much enjoyed his feeling of superiority as a man and he belittled the powers of the feminine. He had often put down his wife and his daughters. (Indeed my mother never really felt supported or honored for being female, and I suppose this gets handed down through families.) He also communicated that he sorely grieved the deforestation of England and his lack of connection to natural law that was lost with the onslaught of Christianity. I was surprised but touched by his intense sharing.

In the garden in Swansea I met with my own grandmother, Jane Evans. She, who had been a born-again Christian, told me that she grieved her rigidity and judgments. She realized that the divine power of healing is not restricted to one path of human belief. She told me that she had interpreted her belief in Jesus and healing in too narrow a way. She honored my way and she was very proud of the divine feminine knowledge of herbs and healing passed on through the females of her family. She had been a faith healer, and she was glad to give me her blessing now that she had a higher perspective. She was happy to see that my energetic healing work and my astrological and tarot guidance had helped so many people. I was thrilled to receive her recognition and experience her broader perspective.

Then the bees brought both of my lineage lines together in a chalice of the divine feminine that magically appeared in my hands, and from the cup grew a beautiful tree. Both families gave me the words "ancient sovereignty." These words gave me a connection back to the lands of the British Isles and the trees and Celtic ways. I felt encouraged to keep working with the trees, and to share what I have learned of Celtic cosmology and the Celtic tree calendar.

Much to my surprise, it seems that the dead are as interested in healing, growth, and consciousness as many of the living are. My loved ones wanted to tell me that they had changed. That they were more conscious. That they had learned a thing or two! This was a guided journey that provided healing not only to me, but to my family lineages. Miracles do occur.

When you come to the thirteenth moon month and consider the teachings of Elder, think about your loved ones that have crossed the veil, as well as your ancestors. Write them letters. Call them close. They may have similar stories to share about how they have changed. Every change in consciousness can be healing for a lineage.

Think about the wisdom teachings of the Elder and her totems, guides, and deities. Think about endings and new beginnings. As this ends the Celtic year, it can be a time of letting go. Let go of regrets, mistakes, and any sense of failure. Consider cutting loose any unfinished projects or negative thoughts or behavior patterns. Time to sweep the garden clean and allow it to rest while dreaming of new adventures and plans.

It can be a time to refocus and set new intentions. It may be a time to seek the advice of an elder or to record an elder's story if you are still lucky enough to have such a person in your life. If you are an elder yourself, do not be afraid to share your wisdom.

KOAD–GROVE–DAY
October 31

Ogham: The Koad: ✕

Keywords: The grove, the temple, the silence, the void, initiation, re-connection with spirit, communicating with and appreciating the dead, recommitment to your spiritual path

Totems: Your personal totems

Guides and Deities: Your personal guides and deities, Crone Goddesses, ancestors and loved ones that have passed over, Hecate (Greek), Cerridwen, Holle (Germany)

Practical Guidance: The veil between the worlds is thin. Pay attention to impressions, intuitions, dreams, visions, and synchronicities. Those beyond the veil may be trying to contact you.

Koad/Grove/Day Ceremony

Holiday
Samhain, Hallowmas, Halloween is October 31.

Please note that on this day you can either choose to use the Koad ceremony or to use the Samhain ceremony since they fall on the same day and have similar themes. The Koad celebration marks the end of the Celtic tree calendar and completes the tree theme. The Koad or the Grove, the Day, represents the act of making space to communicate with Source and our personal guides and totems. Koad lends itself to a solo ceremony of gratitude. This is the day to take time out from our busy lives, and sit in silence.

Samhain marks the six-week sun position on the Wheel of the Year between the autumn equinox and the Winter Solstice and marks the ending of the seasonal Celtic year. On this holiday we remember and communicate with our ancestors and our unseen helpers in the realms of mystery.

Purpose

To celebrate the Grove. To unite with the oneness, universal wisdom, and unity consciousness. To renew our spiritual path and understanding. To communicate with the otherworld and seek courage and guidance from our ancestors and our loved ones who have passed over. We contemplate passing over the threshold.

Preparation

Have some incense ready to light within a holder or abalone dish. Make copies of the "We Are a Circle" chant included on page 219. You will need a bowl or cauldron of soil, one large central candle, and smaller candles for your participants to light. You will need a translucent bowl filled with water that is easy to pass from one person to another, and a flashlight.

Welcome and Greetings

Welcome to our Grove ceremony. Introduce yourself and go around the circle having each participant share their name and why they came to the circle. Have them close their eyes and share a moment of silence to prepare for the ceremony.

Call the Directions

Call the directions and invite in the energies of the Grove and your own personal totems, guides, and deities. This is a day to honor our helpers. We give our gratitude for their support and guidance. This is the time of year when we contact loved ones who have crossed over, spirits, ancestors, and the group mind of our clan. This marks the end of the year, when we let go of outdated ideas and influences and prepare for new beginnings in November. We honor the crone aspect of the Goddess.

Teachings

The Grove was our ancestors' church. In Britain, the Grove was called the *nemeton*, and in Ireland it was called the *fidnemed*. The ancients met in the Grove to give gratitude and to hold their ceremonies and festivals and celebrations as they moved through the seasons and the Wheel of the Year. The Grove was a sacred place or sanctuary, and an enclosure for the gathering place of powerful spirits and entry into the Annwn, the spirit world. These groves often sat upon natural springs and were enclosed or marked by circular or square trenches or fences. The goddess of the sacred grove was named Nemetona. Often local gods and goddesses were invoked as well.

We celebrate this last day of the Celtic year as a time-out space. We call it The Day. It also represents any time that you choose to set aside for meditation, ritual, or ceremony. It is a time to renew your commitment to your spiritual path. This is your inner door to the mysteries. It is your sacred path. It is your own phone line to the ancestors and to their guidance. It is the road to our many incarnations.

We die and are reborn. It is the teaching that death is not to be feared. Death is a portal to new dimensions of experience, soul growth, and spiritual evolution. This is a special threshold for communication between the seen and unseen realms as well as higher dimensions of love and light.

This is a day that represents an initiatory passage through death and rebirth. It represents a "mystical death" that is an important part of every transcendent/ecstatic experience and spiritual transformation. It is a powerful element of shamanistic traditions all over our world.

This day represents unlimited potential, open possibilities, and all that is. It is the unnameable face of the god or the goddess. It is all-magical and all-powerful.

See this day as a day of transformation. This day encourages us to drop ego and embrace our identification with spirit. We identify with our essential self that never dies. We are no longer afraid of death. When we enter our light body, we become one with the regenerative power of the mysteries. We converse with our higher selves.

See yourself as an initiate of the Grove. To undergo a mystical death/ rebirth trance journey includes elements of dismemberment, reintegration and transformation. In the process, one receives the gifts of magical tools for healing and shamanic practice. These tools include songs, stories, poems, symbols, allies, and guides. As we enter inner space we gain mythical awareness. This is a time for self-initiation.

Chant

> What is the teaching of the Grove? Love is our birthright.
> Our freedom comes from remembering our true essence.
> Behold! We are spiritual beings having a human experience.
> And we are free to communicate with our loved ones and ancestors.
> We seek to understand and participate in the mysteries.
> What is the teaching of the Grove?
> Higher consciousness and unity.

Sing

Choose songs that honor the mystery, ancestors, and the divine.

Read

> Honoring the crone.
> This is the night of our crone.
> She is our ancient medicine woman.

She is a hag, a mother, and a maiden.
She is our shape-shifter.
This is the time of our crone.
She is our midwife at our birth.
She is our escort at our death.
She leads us into every transformation.
This is the night when the veil is thin.
The doorways between the worlds are open.
She holds the lantern.
She lights the way.
She stands behind us in the darkness.
As we scry for her touch.
She serves us all with love.
She is our antidote for our sorrows.
She reminds us that there is nothing to fear.
She helps us to trust the dark.
She fashions us a boat to travel through the mystery.
She is the beginning and she is the end.
She is our own ancient dark lady.
We greet her with love.

Guided Meditation

Close your eyes and place your attention on your breath. Let go of worldly concerns and breathe slowly and deeply as you enter a quiet space within. Simply allow yourself to just be, as you travel deeply within yourself ... (pause)

You find yourself in the middle of a great forest. It is a cool autumn day and the leaves are falling from the trees. You find yourself enclosed within a grand Grove. The trees are bright with their red and golden leaves. They sway in the gentle wind. Take a moment to notice the Grove and feel the wind upon your face. Smell the autumn scents of the forest. Above the Grove you see wispy white clouds traveling across the blue sky. You feel welcomed and at home here.

Take a moment to feel the strength, protection, and sacred space offered by this Grove...You move to the center and find yourself holding a basket full of the stems and leaves of the fifteen trees we have worked with over the year. You sit down upon an altar cloth spread on the ground and you place the many leaves around you. You give your gratitude for their grace and teaching.

From the edges of the Grove, a grand elder comes forward. She is dressed in a long forest green cape and the edges of her silver hair show from beneath her hood. She is ancient yet young. Her body moves with grace and aliveness. Her face is radiant, and she comes closer to you. Her smile is infectious, and you feel a deep sense of well-being in her presence. She beckons you to stand, and she takes your hand. She is the grand dame crone, the midwife of death and rebirth. She knows you well as she tracks your life choices. She is glad to have this moment with you on this magnificent portal day.

She is here to cut and reap what you no longer need. Let her take that which is ready to go: burdens, sorrows, regrets, denials, grudges, disappointments, procrastinations...Allow her to take the whole year and cut it away as you prepare for the new. She will harvest the energy and return it to you for the new. She reminds you that every moment is the beginning of a new story. (Pause)

She places her hand on your heart. At that moment the wind rushes through the Grove and the trunks of the trees sway and the leaves and branches seem to have a language of their own. Let them speak to you. All their messages from the mystery come to you. Allow the strength and power and magic to enter. Listen to what the trees have to say.

Your own guides may show up. What do they share with you? Here you can touch truth and wisdom. Here you can regain your power and determination. Let it be so...

This is your special Grove and you can return anytime you want to. All they require is that you enter and let your fears go. The Grove invites you into the silence. Here you meet up with your intuition, your dreams, your visions, and your aspirations. Look around you and give your Grove your gratitude. Thank the crone. Thank your helpers.

Know that you are cleansed and purified. You are reborn. You are brand new. You are ready to enter the new year and create a whole new story on a whole new level. Begin to return to the here and now slowly. When are ready, open your eyes. Ground and center.

Sharing

Have the group share their experiences from the Grove meditation.

Activity: Scrying

Scrying is an ancient method of communicating with the mystery. Looking into a bowl of water or a mirror with unfocused eyes often brings visions and impressions. We enter a portal into the mystery and we can see, hear, know, feel, sense, and imagine messages from our loved ones, our guides, and our totems. I like to do this in the dark with a translucent bowl filled with water and have a flashlight or light source under the bowl as I pass it around to my participants.

Say: "This day is set aside for communicating with the unseen realm. Within that realm rests our regeneration and renewal. This is your time to receive messages that you require."

Turn off the lights and pass the scrying bowl around with a candle or a small flashlight held underneath it to illuminate the water. Have a time of silence for each person to look in deeply. Play some meditative music as the bowl is passed around.

Sharing

After everyone has had a chance, pass the talking stick and allow them to share what they saw or heard or envisioned.

Read

Honoring the ancients.
We circle around the center.
We call in the spirits of our loved ones.

We feel their loving presence.
We offer them our prayers of gratitude.
We circle around the center.
We call in the spirits of the ancient ones.
We feel their loving wisdom and truth.
We offer them our prayers of gratitude.
We circle around the center.
We call in our spirit totems, guides, and deities.
We feel their loving support and guidance.
We offer them our prayers of gratitude.
We circle around the center.
We call in the spirits of the trees.
We feel their grace and protection.
We offer them our prayers of gratitude.
To the unseen realm where we come from.
And where we will return.
We depend on you as our source.
You feed our intelligent hearts.
You guide our way.
You write in our soul's journey book.
We feel your love.
We give our gratitude.
(Light incense)
And so, we send our prayers with the rise of this smoke.
And so it is. Blessed be.

Sing

Choose a song that invokes the mystery.

Activity: Honoring the Mystery

Turn off the lights. Light the central candle in a large earthen container
with soil in it. Go around and have your participants light a smaller can-

dle from the central candle and place theirs in the soil. Have the group listen to music as they contemplate the mystery.

Chant

When all have lit and placed their candles, have the circle stand. Pass out copies of the following chant. Chant and repeat three times together:

> We are a circle
> We enter the void and let go of what has been created
> We herald in the light as we die and are reborn
> We create but again a new story
> The end is our beginning
> And the beginning is the end
> We are a circle
> Never-ending
> We honor the mystery

Sing

Choose an ending song that has to do with our ancestors, the crone, or entering the darkness.

Ending

Place prayers for loved ones into the center. Give gratitude to the ancestors and your loved ones who have passed over. Give gratitude to this dark time of year and to the crone. Imagine your own inner bonfire. Take a moment to throw all that you no longer need onto it and watch it as the flames grow larger. Watch as the flame consumes that which no longer serves you. Know that you are now ready to begin the new year in a good way. Give gratitude to the Grove. Release the directions and open the circle.

The Grove Story: The Veil Is Thin

When I was in my early thirties, I used to feel totally alone and separated from others. That all changed when I had an opportunity to connect with my relatives that had passed on. I went to see a woman who could communicate with the dead. I was taking a class from her on how to increase my psychic intuition.

She closed her eyes and took a moment to enter a light trance. She began to describe a waiting room that looked like a hallway with two long benches on either side. And the benches were full of people who wanted to talk to me! She invited each of them into the room that we sat in, one at a time.

The first she described was a man with a pipe who only had one leg. He told her that he had diabetes as an older man and had to have the leg amputated at the knee. She asked me if I knew such an older gentleman with such a leg. "I did," I said. That could describe my grandfather, my dad's dad. I had only met him at the end of his life as he divorced my grandma and left her to take care of her four young children during the Depression years. He was a traveling salesman. I met him right before he died; I guess he showed up to make amends. We had always thought ill of him, I would say, shirking his responsibilities and leaving my dad to grow up without a father's influence. My grandmother had struggled financially to raise her children. There was a family wound there.

The woman shared with me what he told her. First, he wanted me to know that he loved me and my son very much and that he watched out for us. I had taken photos that had a strange white shape in them—he told me that was him. (Indeed, I had three photos like this.) He said he was always very close to me and was my guardian angel. When I needed special advice and a warning, he sent me the message three times. I thought about it, and I did have to agree that in times of trouble I often heard the same words of advice or warning three times.

He also asked my forgiveness. He said there was a side to the story of his life with my grandmother that I had not heard. "Okay, what was it?" He said that he had made a mistake (I imagine that was an affair). He asked my grandmother for forgiveness and told her how sorry he was. She grew bitter and resentful and never let him forget it. She held his mistake over him. He wanted to make his marriage work and they had another baby. But eventually, he said (admitting to his weakness, or his pride), she could not move past her resentment or her withholding and he gave up. He found love somewhere else. After he divorced he remarried and lived a good life. I did not think to ask him why he didn't help financially support the family though … that was a really hard thing.

Next in came my great-great-grandmother, Claire. She was very strict and came from my mom's side of the family. I recognized her from the reader's description. She told me that even though she seemed overly rule-bound, that she loved that I followed my own heart and my own path and was not locked into convention. That really surprised me because I would have thought she'd be the most judgmental family member of all. She reminded me that she too had gone through a divorce, in a time when that was unusual. She told me to keep on making a life that was my own. She wished that she had.

Next came her sisters, Aunt Maude and Aunt Ruth. I recognized these two from the reader's description. They were just laughing and having a good time. They used to share with us their books about mushroom collecting and rock collecting. They shared with me that they loved that I was interested in so many things and that I took the time to do research and really learn about things I was interested in.

Then came their parents, and their parents before them, and soon the whole room was full of the Mylroie and Corneleus families. They all sent me much love. And I felt it.

When the session was over, I felt full. And I felt like I would never feel totally alone ever again because I have a whole waiting room of relatives and ancestors who were my fans and my cheerleaders. They hoped that I would do what I needed to live a full and fulfilled life, and that I wouldn't hold myself back for lack of support, or because of convention, or because I didn't pay attention to my own passions and my own heart.

The celebration of Samhain always confronts me with the reality of death. I have come a long way in my understanding of life and death and communication across the veil. And I have had many unexplained experiences. I have learned that our dead want to communicate with us. This was a strong Celtic belief. This communication was a source of support and renewal for the living.

And so, at this time of year, at Samhain, I think of those that have passed on and I know that communication is possible. I think of my parents and my relatives and of my dearly missed friends. I place pictures of my loved ones and of my loved animals upon my altar to draw them closer. I give gratitude for everything about the people I miss.

Whether we die in our sleep, suddenly in an unexpected accident, through a violent act of war or crime, through illness, or through our own hands ... I do not put my attention there. I know that the dead do not die; they change form. Consciousness is ongoing. I choose to believe that death is simply a door. I believe that door leads us back into an expanded awareness of consciousness and love.

This is a day for you to take a time-out and contemplate the mysteries. This is a portal for you to seek guidance from those who have gone before you and returned home. Your ancestors and loved ones are very close. Invite them in. Sit quietly and let them whisper their messages to you.

This is a portal in which you can review your spiritual understanding of who you truly are and what your purpose is. If you have no idea, simply sit quietly and allow and invite spirit to share with you. This universal loving consciousness will attend to you and imbue you with courage and light if you but ask.

It is a day to think about the meaning of death. The teaching is not to fear the transition. You are never alone and always supported. The Grove teaches that there is no ending. There is no death. There is spiritual evolution as we die and are reborn, as we incarnate, or ascend. And before we choose our next destination, while we are in spirit we come to fully understand that we are multidimensional beings that can travel the universe of worlds and galaxies and spiritual dimensions. We are dancing in the great mystery of our cosmos and beyond.

Rest in the Grove. Get out in nature and be with the forest. She will hold you well. She will renew you and reassure you. Give your gratitude for all that is!

Samhain Ceremony
October 31

Samhain is the most important holiday in the Wheel of the Year. It marks the beginning of the dark half of the year. Samhain is a portal in which the veil between the realms is very thin. It is a time to honor our beloved dead and ancestors and to contemplate the concepts of reincarnation and the transmigration of the soul. It is a time when we seek to receive messages and insight from the spiritual realms. We do not deny that we grieve for those who have passed on, and yet we understand that there is the continuation of life in the spirit realm. This is part of the regeneration promised within the mystery.

Purpose

To celebrate Samhain.

Preparation

Have your participants bring pictures of loved ones and pets who have passed on.

Welcome and Greetings

Welcome to our Samhain ceremony. Introduce yourself and go around the circle having each participant share their name and why they came to the circle. Have them close their eyes and share a moment of silence to prepare for the ceremony.

Call the Directions

Call in the directions and energies of Samhain.

Teachings

Samhain represents an ending and a beginning, and it is the day that we remember our dead and seek communication. We give our gratitude for their help, for their guidance, and for their protection. We remember. The ancients held their ceremonies within special groves. The energy developed over time at these sacred sites offered enhanced communication with loved ones and ancestors that resided in the otherworld.

Here in this place and on this day, we choose to interact with the mystery. We make time to meditate in the silence. We enter the void where all is created. We let go of our grievances and allow the light to replace our regrets, resentments, and old stories of pain. We release worn-out perceptions, ideals, values, and plans. We open to the new.

This is a day to give your gratitude to what has been, and to thank our personal totems, guides, and deities as well as the tree spirits that have informed you throughout the Celtic year. We honor the Goddess in her many forms, but especially the crone aspect. We honor our loved ones that have passed on.

Chant

What is the teaching of Samhain? The veil is thin.
Our wisdom and regeneration come from embracing
the great mystery.
Behold! Our Crone Goddess leads the way to the otherworld.
And we are free to commune with our loved ones who have
passed through the veil.
We seek their love and guidance.
What is the teaching of Samhain? Death is merely a doorway
between the worlds.

Read

Tonight is also a night of remembrance. There are many nature people who honored the sun, the moon, and the stars, and followed the seasonal celebrations and honored the mysteries. And many were hunted and killed for their beliefs. In medieval times, many lost their lives and were labeled as witches.

Tonight, we honor those who have died and suffered at the hands of oppression for their beliefs. Take a moment to remember the burning times and those ancestors of Europe who were killed during the holocaust of the nature peoples.

Many have suffered great oppression. We remember you. We remember the innocent. We remember you who died in the burning times. You who died in the flames that seared your flesh. You who were gagged and drowned in the water. You who died under the piles of stones crushing you. You who were tortured and broken. We remember you.

We remember all of those living and dead who have suffered in the name of oppression. May your raging, howling, crying spirits know peace and join us tonight as we honor you who have gone before us, who have paved the way and created our freedom with your sacrifices. We bless you our ancestors, who aspired for freedom. We meditate on your sacrifice.

(Play some music as they sit in the silence. This is a powerful way to honor the native European nature people who were killed as witches during the Middle Ages.)

Activity: Honoring the Oppressed

Ask your participants to take a moment to remember all of the people around the globe who have been conquered by another people and been forced to give up their worldview, their way of life, their language, and their unique form of spirituality.

Stand together in your circle and join hands. Have everyone close their eyes.

Say: "Let us create a vision together of a world that honors diversity, celebrates difference, and works together to honor the earth and all her life-forms. See the elders of all cultures on the globe being honored. See indigenous people respected for their wisdom and knowledge. Take a moment to see this and to infuse this with light and life."

Go around the circle and have the participants call out the names of those who have been oppressed.

Go around the circle and ask them to make prayers for all oppressed people.

Sing

Choose a song that honors the ancestors. "Blood of the Ancients" by Ellen Klavor is a good one and you can find it on the internet.

Read

> Tonight we honor our own dead. You who have passed on to the otherworld—ancestors, daughters, mothers, grandmothers, sons, fathers, grandfathers, lovers, friends, and pets —we remember you. Take a moment to think about these ancestors, relatives, friends, and pets who have passed on. (Pause)

Sing

Choose songs that speak about the ancestors.

Read

> Listen for the whispers of the ancestors.
> They speak to us.
> Their song is in the fire's crackle.
> Their tears are in the rain on the windowpane.
> Their praises are the sun on our face.
> They are here with us.
> They speak to us.
> Their words are in the rustling of the leaves.
> Their encouragements in the wind rippling through the grass.
> Their laughter is in the play of our children.
> They are here with us.

They speak to us.

They are alive within our inner world.

They are alive within our friends and family.

They bless us with the turning of the seasons.

They are here with us.

Although we live in different realms

They are not dead to us.

They are with us every day and every night.

They love us best.

They have never left us.

And they will greet us with love.

When it is our turn to pass through the veil.

Guided Meditation

(Turn off the lights.) Close your eyes and settle into the darkness. Breathe deeply into a quiet space. Just be with your breath as you move deeper and deeper into the silence. Just allow the quiet softness to envelop you as you let go of any stress, worry, or concern. Breathe even more deeply into the simple act of doing nothing as you enter this quietness.

You are about to enter a vortex of power. This is a place beyond imagining where birth and death, dark and daylight, and joy and pain meet. You are about to step between the worlds, beyond time and outside the realm of your human life … (pause)

You find yourself at the entrance to a grotto or cave. You do not enter but you know that there is much energy here and you feel a sense of anticipation. Soon you notice that people are beginning to come out of the cave. They are dressed in their best clothing, but from many different times in history. You see that a circle of people is forming around you.

Those standing in front of you are family members that have passed over. You can feel them sending you love and encouragement, so there is no fear here. Next to your parents or aunts and uncles are your grandparents, and next to them your great-grandparents, and other relatives, and so on as the circle enlarges to include your ancestors. You feel an overwhelming sense of protection and joy. They are all feeding you with appreciation. You are their living power and proof. You have all their dreams standing upon your shoulders and so you are their fulfillment. Give your gratitude. You carry their best hopes and aspirations and they are delighted to support you here. Take a moment to receive their messages. (Long pause)

Your pets will probably show up as well. They are so very happy to see you and interact with you. They send you a blast of love and you return this. Listen to their barks and meows and the sounds of birds and other animals you have cared for. Can you feel their gratitude? Know that they are here and that they do communicate with you. Are you willing to hear them and listen? Take a moment with this... Send them your love and appreciation. Think of the happy times that you shared. Feel your love and affection for them that you still hold strong in your heart. (Long pause)

Now you notice people coming into the circle that represent the next generation. These may be your own children, or children that you love and teach and influence, or your grandchildren or great-grandchildren. They could be your nieces and nephews and their children. Notice that there is a growing number of people joining you who are coming from the future. Send them love and encouragement. Send them your messages. What is it that you think is essential for their well-being, and for the well-being of the planet? Send them a blast of love.

Those of the past leave the outer circle to return to the cave that leads back to the otherworld. They will greet you and help you when it is your turn to walk over the threshold. The animals return as well but you feel their love. The relatives and loved ones of the future dissolve back into the ethers. You feel great love for them and for their aspirations and choices. You feel immense encouragement to be so connected to your own lineage. Breathe this in. (Long pause)

Now focus on yourself. Look at your life. Take stock... Are you happy with where you are and what you are doing? What would you like to accomplish or receive or manifest for your next year of life? Just be here with these thoughts as you contemplate another year's passing. Allow the love here to fill you and motivate you and protect you.

When you are ready, say your goodbyes and know that you are never really separated from these souls. Begin to gently come back to the room. When you are ready, open your eyes. Give your gratitude. Ground and center.

Sharing

Have your participants share their experiences from the journey. What was it like to receive the love from their ancestors, and to send it toward their future relatives? What changes do they have to make to allow for a greater expression in the future year of who they are and what they want to accomplish?

Sing

Choose a song that honors the ancestors.

Sharing

The circle can talk about the pictures they brought and any special memories they want to share about their loved ones and pets that have crossed over.

Sing

Choose closing songs such as "May the Circle Be Open," "Merry Meet," or "We Are a Circle."

Ending

Give your gratitude for this special day and for the Grove. Thank the
ancestors and loved ones that have passed on and the pets that we miss.
Thank them for their guidance and love. Thank those who walk into
the future. Make prayers for the planet and for healing. Make prayers to
take care of the earth. Open the circle and release the directions.

CONCLUSION

It is my greatest hope that you, the reader, may use these ceremonies to build you relationship with the trees of the Celtic tree calendar and to enhance your communication with the healing power of the unseen realm that loves us. It is my greatest dream that you may experience the power, love, and guidance that is offered within these tree teachings. And I so hope that the stories demonstrate to you just how the unseen realm communicates with us, and how our ancestors and those who have passed over are on our healing team. The spirit of the trees and plants, and their totems, guides, and deities are real, and ready to offer their service as we invite them to do so.

I hope you will find direction for creating your own experiences, because that is indeed what fuels us. Actual experience with divinity—with the higher spiritual realms of love and light—is what expands us and grows us and moves us beyond our fears. The loving contact that is encouraged by this teaching allows the spirit realm to share healing with you and increase your own inspiration, creativity, joy, and personal expression—leading to a fulfilled life.

It also offers you ways to navigate troubled waters. It offers you a template for how to live well on the planet and reminds you to never take for granted what is given to us so freely—the air, the water, the sun, and our Mother Earth. I pray that we all become better stewards for this paradise that we have been gifted.

I encourage you to foster your gratitude. And in conclusion, I ask you to take care of our tree friends, who provide us with so much, even beyond the very air that we breathe. Perhaps this world that we call reality is only a dream, and what we call the "real world" is less real, and ultimately less powerful, than the unseen realm. We may be just a mere reflection of that perfection. That mystery is unsolvable, but may this cosmic view organized into the Celtic tree calendar provide you with a way to journey through each year of your life with gratitude and an open heart and mind—appreciative of nature, our world, and the universe we live in. I hope this work increases your sense of wonder and gratitude, and that it helps you to experience the magnitude and perfection of the cosmos, as well as your connection to the great universal mind of love and higher consciousness.

APPENDIX A

The Principles of Manifestation

1. Each of us is a cocreator in the universe. The tools that we possess—action, word, thought—give us the abundant ability of creation.

2. We say, "I am." Not "I want" or "I need" or "I wish." The universe itself replies and grants us the waiting, needing, or wishing. Say out loud: "I am creating..." or "I am manifesting..." and feel the universe respond.

3. The words you speak are powerful. If you state what you are creating or manifesting as an absolute truth, your words are more than idle wishes. For example, "I am creating a life of joy" or "I am manifesting peace and kindness." Envision these truths over and over; they must be possible and true to you. Fill the words with passion; channel every emotion into these statements. Accept this construction without reserve. Speak it aloud. Then let it go. You will be surprised. Say, "For the highest good of all involved, this or better. If it harms none, so be it!"

4. Act as though it has already come to be. See it in your mind's eye having already happened—you are enjoying the fruits of your labor. Your joy provides the fuel for what you are creating. Continuously envision yourself in your mind's eye, successfully manifesting that which you desired to create.

5. Maintain your original intention. Each time you change your mind, even momentarily or based upon your mood, the universe has to adjust its flow to accommodate the change. Practice holding your intention, just as you would practice meditating. If you lose focus, gently nudge yourself back to your original intention.

6. Firm resolve in what you give your energy to is key. If fear or doubts show up, gently and kindly put them to bed. Tell yourself that you cannot fail. This won't be easy; it takes discipline and practice to change a negative thought, word, or action into a positive one. When you change your vibration, you also change what you attract into your life. It's that simple.

7. The universe is happiest to offer its support if your goal also has a higher purpose that heals or benefits others, or that works for the good of all.

8. Remember the old Buddhist saying: "Fall down seven times, get up eight." Don't be discouraged. Keep moving toward your goals.

9. Take a practical, step-by-step approach to manifesting your goals and desires. Rather than focusing on what we wish for or long to be, build the foundation that supports transformation. It's much easier to create a new life, a new job, a new relationship if we are practical and do one step at a time.

10. If what you're doing isn't working, try the opposite. If you're going crazy working hard to make something happen and it's not working, do nothing instead. If you aren't doing anything to promote manifestation, do at least one thing. If you're only thinking, start writing the thoughts down—then share them, say them aloud, and act on them.

11. Find someone to share with. Finding an encouraging partnership can be very beneficial. Set timelines. Have someone there to hear you speak your intention of what you desire to manifest, and then work on a set of steps together.

12. What you desire to desist persists. Rather than obsessing over the things you do not want, focus on the things you do want to manifest. Feed what you want to grow and stop feeding what you don't.

13. Maintain clear thoughts and visualizations. Stay focused on your feelings and clearly picture yourself being successful in your goal. Revel in the feelings of victory and the mental images of your positive outcome. This is key to manifestation.

APPENDIX B
Music

I have learned many songs in women's circles that I have participated in for years and I am not sure of their origin. Many I have learned from CDs and I have listed them here. I have placed an asterisk next to those that I think will be most helpful. They are excellent sources. If you want just one song, many can be downloaded from the internet or Amazon.

CDs

Ani Williams, *Magdalene's Gift, Songs to the Beloved, Sisters of the Dream, Songs of the Jaguar, Children of the Sun,* and *Wind Spirit*

Brooke Medicine Eagle, *A Gift of Song* and *For My People*

*Charlie Murphy and Jami Sieber, *Canticles of Light*

Dawn L. Ferguson, *Heartsongs of the Universe*

David and Steve Gordon, *Misty Forest Morning*

Enya, *The Memory of Trees*

*Flight of the Hawk, *Shamanic Songs and Ritual Chants*

Florence Lorraine Bayes, *In All Her Fullness*

*Jennifer Berezan, *Praises for the World*

*Libana, *The Circle is Cast*

Lisa Thiel, *Vocation of the Graces*

Medwyn Goodall, *Medicine Woman*

*Moving Breath, *She Changes: A Collection of Songs from Healing Circles*

Nakai, *Earth Spirit*

Performers at the Women of Wisdom Conference in Seattle, *Wisdom of Women Collection, Empowering the Dreams & Spirit of Women*

*Reclaiming and Friends, *Chants: Ritual Music*

Robert Grass & Women on Wings of Song, *Ancient Mother*

Shawna Carol, *Mystic Soul: Songs of Celebration* and *Goddess Chant: Sacred Pleasures*

She Carries Me, *Returning*

Suggested Songs

Here is a list of songs and ways that you can find them. It is to your advantage to collect the words and make copies of your songs to pass out for your circles and ceremonies. You can look them up on the internet by title or author or by the CD mentioned. You can also look up women's circle songs, Pagan songs, and nature songs.

For Calling in Spirit

"Listen, Listen, Listen to my Heart Song" (a Paramahansa Yogananda chant)

"Oh, Great Spirit, Earth, Sun, Sky and Sea. You are inside and all around me" (a Native American chant by Adele Getty)

"Oh, Great Spirit I'm Calling on You" (on the *Flight of the Hawk* CD)

"Spirit Above Me" (words set to traditional music by Mujiba Cabugos)

For Creativity

"Spiraling into the Center" (by Lorna Kohler, on the *Flight of the Hawk* CD)

"There's a River of Birds in Migration" (on the *Libana* CD)

"We All Come from the Goddess" (traditional, on the *She Changes* CD
    by Moving Breath)

"We are the Weaver. We are the Web" (traditional, by Starhawk)

For Honoring the Ancestors

"It's the Blood of the Ancients" (by Ellen Klaver, on the Charlie
    Murphy CD and on the internet)

"Like the Old Ones Gone Before" (on the *She Changes* CD)

"Old Ones Hear Us" by Mujiba Cabugos

"We Are the Old Ones" (on the *Flight of the Hawk* CD)

For Honoring the Earth

"All My People" by Brooke Medicine Eagle

"I Walk Your Sacred Ground" by Brooke Medicine Eagle

"Mother I Feel You" by Diane Martin and Windsong

"Where I Sit Is Holy" by Adele Getty

For Honoring the Goddess

"We All Come from the Goddess" (traditional)

"The River Song" by Diana Hildebrand-Hull

"Blood of the Ancients" by Ellen Klavor

"Honored Maiden Huntress" (traditional, on the *She Changes* CD)

"Changing Woman" by Adele Getty

"Isis, Astarte, Diana" by Deena Metzger

"She's Been Waiting" (traditional, by Paula Wallowitz on the
    She Changes CD)

For Honoring the Mystery

"Oh, Great Spirit, Earth, Sun, Sky and Sea. You are inside and all around me" (a Native American chant by Adele Getty)

"Oh, Great Spirit I'm Calling on You" (on the *Flight of the Hawk* CD)

"Sweet Surrender" (on the *Flight of the Hawk* CD)

"There Is a Secret One Inside" (from poem by Kabir, Tr. Robert Bly)

"Where I Sit is Holy" by Adele Getty

For Honoring Trees

"Oh, Cedar Tree" by Joseph Hillaire

For Meditating

"The Light in the Mystery" or "The Song of Remembrance" (on the *She Changes* CD)

For Honoring the Elements

"Earth Our Body" (traditional, on the *She Changes* CD)

"The earth, the air, the fire the water, return, return, return, return" (by Starhawk on *Chants: Ritual Music* CD)

For Healing

"Like the Old Ones" (on the *She Changes* CD)

"Old Ones Hear Us" by Mujiba Cabugos

"Spirit Above Me" (on the *She Changes* CD)

Ending Songs

"May the Circle Be Open" (traditional)

"Merry Meet" (traditional)

"We Are a Circle" by Rick Hamouris

For the Holidays

For Winter Solstice

"I Walk Your Sacred Ground" by Brooke Medicine Eagle

"Light is Returning" by Charlie Murphy

"Old Ones Hear Us" by Mujiba Cabugos

For Imbolc

"Sweet Surrender" (on the *Flight of the Hawk* CD)

"The River Song" by Diana Hilderbrand-Hull

"We all Come from the Goddess" (traditional)

For Spring Equinox

"Mother I Feel You" by Diane Martin and Windsong

"Oh, Great Spirit, Earth, Sun, Sky and Sea. You are inside and all around me" (a Native American chant by Adele Getty)

"Spirit above Me" (on the *She Changes* CD)

For Beltane

I really like to use the poem "The Charge of the Goddess" (traditional), which can be found online, or on Jennifer Berezan's CD, *She Carries Me, #1: She Who Hears the Cries of the World*. This is such an excellent invocation for calling on the Great Mother and I highly recommend it. Or play "Sacred Pleasures" by Shawna Carol on her CD, *Goddess Chant*.

"The earth, the air, the fire the water, return, return, return, return" (by Starhawk on *Chants: Ritual Music* CD)

"Where I Sit is Holy" by Adele Getty

"We All Come from the Goddess" (traditional)

For Summer Solstice

"I Walk Your Sacred Ground" by Brooke Medicine Eagle

"Sweet Surrender" (on the *Flight of the Hawk* CD)

"We are All One with the Infinite Sun Forever and Ever and Ever" (traditional)

For Lammas

"Secret One Inside" (from a poem by Kabir, Tr. Robert Bly)

"The River Song" by Diana Hilderbrand-Hull

"We all Come from the Goddess" (traditional)

For Fall Equinox

"Om Tare Tuttare Soha" (This is a chant from Tibet. You can find it on the internet.)

"The earth, the air, the fire, the water, return, return, return, return" by Starhawk

"We are the Old Ones" (on the *Flight of the Hawk* CD)

For Samhain

Play a recording of "The Burning Times" by Charlie Murphy. You can download it from the internet. It is worth your time to do this, as it is a song that will serve you well at this time of year when we remember those who have gone before us.

"The Blood of the Ancients" by Ellen Klavor

"Like the Old Ones Gone Before" (on the *She Changes* CD)

"Old Ones Hear Us" by Mujiba Cabugos

APPENDIX C
More about the Ogham Tree Alphabet

The ogham is an early medieval alphabet developed in the British Isles and it appears on monumental inscriptions dating from the fourth to the sixth century AD, and in manuscripts dating from the sixth to the ninth century AD. It was used mainly to write Primitive and Old Irish, as well as to write Old Welsh, Pictish, and Latin; it was inscribed on stone monuments throughout Ireland (particularly Kerry, Cork, and Waterford) and in England, Scotland, the Isle of Man, and Wales (particularly in Pembrokeshire in South Wales). It is hard to trace the origins of the alphabet because ancient Celtic lore and mythology was never written down but passed on orally. Its origins probably stem from ancient times in the history of the British Isles.

The alphabet consists of a set of straight lines that were etched upon sticks called staves or on stones for markers or monuments. Each line forms a symbol that represents a sigil and letter and can be written vertically (usually read from bottom to top) and horizontally (usually read from left to right). An arrow shaft or some other kind of marking will usually indicate where to begin reading. The markings are made along a stem-line called the druim.

There are many different versions of the ogham tree alphabet, but the one that I use has twenty-five symbols and letters that mostly correspond to a tree or a plant, and the last one represents the sea and has a host of ideas and spiritual meanings—teachings, if you will—that relate to the Celtic cosmology. The use of the ogham has emerged as a powerful modern-day oracle and it has become a valid tool for today's spiritual seekers. Many modern-day Pagans and Wiccans, like myself, have taken to using the ogham as a body of wisdom teaching and can attest to its vibrancy. The twenty-five sigils can be traced, painted, or etched onto staves (wood pieces cut to the same length) and thrown as a divination tool. Sets are also available ready-made on the internet.

The alphabet is divided into the feada (FEHD-uh), which includes the first twenty of the letters, and the forfeda (FOR-fehd-uh), which is the last five. The feada is divided into four groups of five, called aicmes (AYKH-muhs). The first fifteen feada represent the consonants and the last five represent the vowels.

The forfeda, the last five, were added to offer special significance within the system and they represent vowel and consonant combinations. These were added later probably to accommodate Greek and Latin. Each sigil has its own meaning. The first fifteen symbols plus the Koad symbol make up the Celtic tree calendar that I work with.

The Feada

#	LETTER/OGHAM	TREE/ MEANING
	Aicme Beith	
1	┝ B/ Beith	Birch/ Beginning
2	┝ L/ Luis	Rowan/ Protection
3	┝ F, V, GW/ Fearn	Alder/ Guidance

#	Letter/Ogham	Tree/ Meaning
4	𝄆 S/ Saille	Willow/ Feminine Principle
5	𝄆 N/ Nuin	Ash/ World Tree
Aicme Húathe		
6	H / Huathe	Hawthorn/ Cleansing
7	D/ Duir	Oak/ Strength
8	T/ Tinne	Holly/ Justice
9	C/ Coll	Hazel/ Intuition
10	Q/ Quert	Apple/ Choice
Aicme Muin		
11	M/ Muin	Vine/ Prophecy
12	G/ Gort	Ivy/ Labyrinth
13	Ng/ Ngetal	Reed/ Direct Action

#	LETTER/OGHAM	TREE/ MEANING
14	SS, ST, Z/ Straif	Blackthorn/ Negation
15	R/ Ruis	Elder/ Renewal
	Aicme Ailim (Vowels)	
16	+ A / Ailim	Silver Fir/ Foresight
17	O/ Ohn	Gorse/Furze/ Collecting
18	U, W/ Ur	Heather/Mistletoe/ Healing
19	E/ Eadha	White Poplar/Aspen/ Adversity
20	I, J, Y/ Ioho	Yew/ Rebirth

The Forfeda

#	LETTER/OGHAM	TREE/ MEANING
21	✕ EA, CH, KH/ Koad (Shears)	The Grove/ Temple Silence, Intuition
22	◇ OI, TH/ Oir (Helmet)	Spindle/ Fulfillment

#	LETTER/OGHAM	TREE/ MEANING
23	⧢ UI, PE, P/ Uilleand (Bones)	Honeysuckle/ Seeking
24	�␣ IO, PH/ Phagos (Hook)	Beech/ Generations
25	▦ AE, XI, X/ Mor (Weft of the shirt)	The Sea/ Journey, Maternal Links

BiBLiOGRAPHY

Budapest, Zsuzsanna. *The Grandmother of Time*. San Francisco: Harper San Francisco, 1979.

———. *The Holy Book of Women's Mysteries*. Berkeley, CA: Wingbow Press, 1980.

Gadon, Elinor. *The Once and Future Goddess*. San Francisco: Harper and Row Publishers, 1989.

Hidalgo, Sharlyn. *Celtic Tree Oracle*. Victoria, Australia: Blue Angel Publications, 2017.

———. *The Healing Power of Trees: Spiritual Journeys Through the Celtic Tree Calendar*. Woodbury, MN: Llewellyn Publications, 2010.

Jones, Kathy. *The Ancient British Goddess: Her Myths, Legends and Sacred Sites*. Somerset, UK: Ariadne Publications, 1991.

Laxer, Judith. *Along the Wheel of Time: Sacred Stories for Nature Lovers*. Seattle: Booktrope Editions, 2014.

Leek, Sybil. *A Ring of Magic Islands*. Garden City, NY: American Photographic Book Publishing Co., 1976.

McColman, Carl. *The Complete Idiot's Guide to Celtic Wisdom*. New York: Alphy, a division of Penguin, 2003.

Murry, Liz, and Colin Murry. *The Celtic Tree Oracle: A System of Divination*. New York: St. Martin's Press, 1988.

Rudhyar, Dane. *An Astrological Mandala: The Cycle of Transformations and Its 360 Symbolic Phases*. New York: Random House, 1973.

Starhawk, *The Spiral Dance*. San Francisco: Harper and Row, 1979.

Stein, Diane. *Casting the Circle: A Women's Book of Ritual*. Freedom, CA: The Crossing Press, 1990.

To Write to the Author

If you wish to contact the author or would like more information about this book, please write to the author in care of Llewellyn Worldwide Ltd. and we will forward your request. Both the author and publisher appreciate hearing from you and learning of your enjoyment of this book and how it has helped you. Llewellyn Worldwide Ltd. cannot guarantee that every letter written to the author can be answered, but all will be forwarded. Please write to:

Sharlyn Hidalgo
℅ Llewellyn Worldwide
2143 Wooddale Drive
Woodbury, MN 55125-2989

Please enclose a self-addressed stamped envelope for reply,
or $1.00 to cover costs. If outside the U.S.A., enclose
an international postal reply coupon.

Many of Llewellyn's authors have websites with additional information and resources. For more information, please visit our website at http://www.llewellyn.com.